Conference on Code Reform

Standards of teaching of foreign codes relating to elementary education, prescribed by Austrian, Belgian, German, Italian and Swiss governments; also the Memorial to the Education Department by the Conference on code reform

Conference on Code Reform

Standards of teaching of foreign codes relating to elementary education, prescribed by Austrian, Belgian, German, Italian and Swiss governments; also the Memorial to the Education Department by the Conference on code reform

ISBN/EAN: 9783337229450

Printed in Europe, USA, Canada, Australia, Japan

Cover: Foto ©Paul-Georg Meister /pixelio.de

More available books at **www.hansebooks.com**

STANDARDS OF TEACHING

OF

FOREIGN CODES

Relating to Elementary Education,

PRESCRIBED BY

AUSTRIAN, BELGIAN, GERMAN, ITALIAN AND SWISS GOVERNMENTS;

ALSO

THE MEMORIAL TO THE EDUCATION DEPARTMENT BY THE CONFERENCE ON CODE REFORM,

WITH THE STANDARDS PROPOSED BY THEM.

WITH AN INTRODUCTION AND NOTES.

BY

A. SONNENSCHEIN.

"What is put into the schools of a country comes out subsequently in the manhood of the nation."—*Stein, quoted by Felkin.*

LONDON:
W. SWAN SONNENSCHEIN & ALLEN.
1881.

TO THE

RIGHT HONOURABLE A. J MUNDELLA, M.P.,

Vice-President of the Committee of Council on Education,

𝔗𝔥𝔦𝔰 𝔙𝔬𝔩𝔲𝔪𝔢

IS, WITH HIS KIND PERMISSION,

RESPECTFULLY INSCRIBED

BY

THE AUTHOR.

LETTER FROM THE RT. HON. A. J. MUNDELLA, M.P., TO THE AUTHOR.

June 14, 1881.

My dear Sir,

I have just received the proof sheets of your work on "Standards of Teaching of Foreign Codes," which you have done me the honour to dedicate to me.

Although I have had barely time to give it a cursory examination, I am able to say that it is an admirable and valuable work, and well worth studying by every friend of popular Education. I hope, indeed, this study will not be limited to the friends of Education, but that many of those who seem to think that we are devoting too much time, labour and money, to this question, will familiarize themselves with its contents. Nothing can be more serviceable to the cause of National Education than that the English people should be accurately informed as to what our neighbours and competitors are doing.

Faithfully yours,
A. J. MUNDELLA.

A. Sonnenschein, Esq.

CONTENTS.

	PAGE
INTRODUCTION	9

STANDARDS FOR ARITHMETIC—

Aargau	25
Alsace-Lorraine	28
Austria	34
City of Bale	35
Bavaria	37
Belgium	38
Canton of Geneva	43
Hamburg	44
Italy	45
Muhlhausen	46
Neuchatel	47
Prussia	50
Saxony	51
Canton de Vaud	52
City of Zurich	54

STANDARDS FOR LANGUAGE—

Aargau	57
Alsace-Lorraine	59
Austria	62
City of Bale	64
Bavaria	66
Belgium	68
Canton of Geneva	77
Hamburg	79
Italy	81
Muhlhausen	82

CONTENTS.

	PAGE
Neuchatel	83
Prussia	92
Saxony	98
Canton de Vaud	102
Zurich	106

STANDARDS FOR GEOGRAPHY—

Aargau	111
Alsace-Lorraine	111
Austria	113
Bavaria	114
Belgium	114
Geneva	118
Hamburg	118
Italy	119
Muhlhausen	120
Neuchatel	121
Prussia	123
Saxony	124
Canton de Vaud	126
Zurich	128

A FEW FOREIGN TIME TABLES	130
THE ENGLISH STANDARDS AND SOME ENGLISH STAGES, WITH COMMENTS	136
MEMORIAL OF THE CONFERENCE ON CODE REFORM	144

INTRODUCTION.

In submitting to my readers the few Courses of Teaching and Standards of Examination which I have at short notice been able to collect, I must crave indulgence for any marks of haste betrayed in this work. I was pressed for time. Between its first conception and its actual appearance, little more than six weeks have elapsed, and only a portion of this short period could I devote to the task I had undertaken.

I also owe some explanation to my readers. The work is necessarily fragmentary, but it is a fragment of a fragment. I have only selected for publication a few subjects from the Standards of a few localities. A work containing all the Standards of all Europe, and also an exhaustive comparison of the provisions of the different Codes, would assume the dimensions of a cyclopædia. Still I hope this little volume will prove of some service to the ever-increasing number of those who are interested in our Elementary Education. I am also anxious to state that I by no means would advise rigorously to follow the footsteps of even the best of these Standards. I am convinced that the energy of intelligence possessed by English children justifies us in making larger strides than some other nations can venture on; but the spirit that dictated these Standards is worthy of our careful study.

I must also point out that the Belgian Standards can be regarded as no more than an aspiration. Up to 1880, the Belgian Government, "according to the law of 1842, did not think it necessary to decree Standards of Study and Examination for the public primary schools. Some large cities, some provincial inspectors, had of their own initiative formulated programmes of study; but in the majority of communes the teachers were the sole interpreters of the intentions of the law on that subject. Experience has condemned this system; wherever the schools have followed some definite plan, the progress has been marked, whilst in the schools left to themselves routine took firm hold."*

These Standards, then, are not yet a year old, and I can only say that the Belgians will be the most enviable of European nations if they reach the goal set before them.

One lesson, however, we can learn from their experience—it is better to have bad Standards than to have no Standards at all. Our own Standards and Stages are bad enough in all conscience; they are meagre, affording no guidance to the teacher; vague, but yet leaving to the teacher no initiative; and their sequence renders good teaching simply impossible, as is shown in the text† (see pp. 136—143), but we rejoice to think that soon we shall be freed from at least this one shackle.

---

* Circular of Mr. Van Humbeck, Belgian Minister of Education, dated 20th July, 1880.

† All that can be urged in favour of such mechanical Standards is, that they supply Inspectors with a "mechanical test," by the "mechanical application" of which they are enabled to escape a thorny responsibility. Yet it would be unwise of the partizans of our present system of inspection if they gave to this plea any prominence, because it opens some very inconvenient questions, such as:

1st. If the "mechanical application of a mechanical test" be an Inspector's principal duty, does it not seem a waste of money and of talent to employ men of high pay, and still higher attainments and culture, in the discharge of functions which might be adequately discharged by a common juryman? Surely it is not of honour and honesty that our University men enjoy a monopoly!

2nd. How is it that Continental Inspectors successfully do face this thorny responsibility? True, their moral responsibility is lighter, because no money grant depends on their report—Payment by Results being a purely English

INTRODUCTION.   11

The reform of our Elementary Education, however, does not mean merely substitution of good for bad Standards. It is the first requisite, no doubt, but only the first, not the sole requisite. Though good teaching and good inspection are incompatible with bad Standards, bad teaching and bad inspection are perfectly compatible with good Standards. The same holds of other provisions of the Code, and practices of the Department. For example: Payment by Results, and exclusion of elementary teachers from the Inspectorate, are practices in which this "always singular nation" stands absolutely alone. Similarly, to set children to teach children has been tried in a few places besides England and abandoned: we still cling to it.* I by no means advocate the total abolition of our Pupil-teacher System, simply because it is impossible; we are so committed to it, it is so interwoven with our whole system of Elementary Education, that the endeavour to tear it out would rend the whole fabric asunder; but a radical reform of it might make it as useful to us as the Proseminary is to Germany.

We accept then thankfully the reform of the Standards as a valuable instalment, but we plead guilty to our gratitude being to some extent "a lively sense of favours to come." For, after

practice; but this is precisely the point on which everything else hinges. To discuss this, means discussing the whole problem of English Elementary Education, which I could not do here without largely exceeding my limits.

I feel safe, however, in prophesying that this cardinal point of the whole Code, this prime source of all our ills, will ere long have to be reconsidered; that we shall with tolerable unanimity arrive at the conclusion that teaching is a spiritual function, and must be judged by the spirit that animates the teacher and pervades his lessons; that it is futile to endeavour to gauge this by any mechanical test, however ingeniously contrived; and that the attempt to evade the thorny responsibility of Inspecting Processes by substituting for it a mere Examination of Results, is nothing less than a dereliction of duty fatal to the best interests of Education.

* France gave the "enseignement mutuel" an exhaustive trial, and has abandoned it; it is still, however, retained in the village schools of Russia, but solely on the plea of poverty.

all, we are in the hands of the Department. In disposing of the grant, it disposes also indirectly of all the moneys raised by rates, school-pence and voluntary subscriptions; if the grant forces the teaching into false grooves, the other resources must follow suit. How important, then, is it that the Department should act with circumspection, wise liberalism and openness to new convictions and reforms! Some believe that it is utopian to hope this.

There are amongst us men of eminence who deny to the State any right to meddle with Education. According to them, the State is as ill fitted to regulate Education as it is ill fitted to regulate Religion; but, these high authorities notwithstanding, the mass of Englishmen, and amongst them the present writer, hold that the State is bound to see to it that the Commonwealth suffer no harm from the ignorance and insensibility of the masses. We are painfully aware that the prosperity of the land, the well-being of each individual inhabitant in it, is staked upon the successful solution of the problem of State-aided Education, and for that very reason we are anxious to define its aims with precision.

The business of State-aided Elementary Education, concisely stated, is the task of "REARING AN INTELLIGENT, MORALIZED POPULATION THAT IS FOND OF READING;" more than that it is as yet impossible to attain, and nothing less than that can or ought to satisfy us. From this it follows directly that it is incumbent on the State to make sure that the teaching for which public money is paid should, *both in matter and in method*, be directed to the attainment of this end.

Now it is clear to everybody who has given thought to the subject, that the prime question in all teaching is not *what* you teach, but *how* you teach it. For the practical utility of most studies is slight when compared with their regenerating and refining influence on the child's character. A man may be a bad reader, writer and computer, and yet a very estimable citizen; whilst a good reader, writer and computer may use these very powers to the detriment of the State. Not so with training;

there the thistle will always bear thistle-seeds, and the fig-tree figs. To training, then, the State must devote its chief attention, and in the selection of the studies this end must be kept primarily in view. Happily for us all, it is easy to combine the utility desired by the practical business man with the higher ends the statesman has in view. We are all agreed that the child must learn reading and writing; it is about the third R that opinions begin to be divided.

A curious superstition—I can call it by no other name—has taken possession of the public mind with respect to the study of Arithmetic or of the Properties of Numbers. Though considered an integral part of a child's education, it is still regarded merely as an *art*, the acquisition of which is indispensable in the affairs of life. Eminent ENGLISH authorities contend that children cannot possibly be made to understand the rationale of arithmetical processes, and that therefore, since taught they must be, they must be taught by rote and not by reason. This is a very sad, but happily, according to the contention of equally eminent English and foreign authorities, a false conclusion. Let us compare the two sister sciences, Geometry, or the study of the properties of SPACE, and Arithmetic, or the study of the properties of TIME. In Geometry not only does nobody venture to propose mere routine teaching, but, spell-bound by Euclid, we insist on deriving, by wonderful tours de force, demonstrations of even the most obvious properties (e.g. Bk. I. Prop. 20) from minima of postulates and axioms. And these demonstrations shall be so irrefragable that the utmost ingenuity of adult Greek sophists shall fail to detect a flaw in them. But in Arithmetic we are bidden to content ourselves with mere conclusions without any demonstration whatsoever. If Euclid were treated in this style, the whole of the First Book could be compressed into one single page. In the one case it is Demonstration, in the other it is Routine, gone mad. If we ask for the reason of this great difference, we are confronted by the unhesitating assertion that Arithmetic is indispensable in the affairs of life, Geometry is not; but as Arithmetic cannot be understood by children, it follows that they must be taught by rote.

In the Standards which I have been enabled to collect, it is Italy alone that keeps these English authorities in countenance; whilst all the other nations, and pre-eminently those that have most distinguished themselves in the field of Education, are most emphatically in the other camp.

But I do not ask my readers to accept the decision of a majority, however weighty and overwhelming it may be; I beg them patiently to examine the case on its own merits.

It is undeniably true that a certain modicum of Arithmetic *is* needed in the affairs of life, but most of us men get on very well with no more than a knowledge of the Four Rules applied to small numbers, a very fragmentary and elementary acquaintance with vulgar fractions, and the vaguest possible insight into the notation of a decimal fraction. Women require still less. How many men or women ever have any need of advanced and complicated notions of fractions, of recurring decimals, of ratios and proportion or of evolution? If we were to confine ourselves to so much study of Arithmetic as most of us are likely to need, our manuals of Arithmetic would shrink to very modest dimensions indeed. The plea of practical usefulness can be and is urged with equal force for several other studies. Why, then, do we of all trades and professions single out that of the accountant as an integral part of our children's curriculum of studies? Is it not because we all feel that there is a training, a discipline, in Arithmetic, which is conferred by no other Elementary Study? But if you give only routine teaching, where is your training? You do not so much as gain an insight into Number, which is the essence of the whole study. At most you train the child into a certain habit of mechanical accuracy. To aim at that, to the neglect of the higher purposes, reminds one of that type of the practical man, the engineer Brindley, who saw in rivers no other use but that "of feeding navigable canals."

I hold, then, that Arithmetic as a science is as indispensable as Reading and Writing; but as a mere art, as a mere series of ingenious tricks and artifices without rhyme or reason, it is of the slightest possible benefit in the school curriculum.

But this training of the intelligence is only a part, and a small part, of the work of a State-aided school; not only mediately through the understanding, but immediately through the emotions, the child's character must be trained, strengthened and developed.

"Surely we *are* by feeling as by knowing;
Changing our hearts, our being changes with them."

Next to Religion, which we cannot touch in our grant-earning schools, there is nothing more formative than Literature,* or an acquaintance with the highest thought and the fairest expression of a nation's mind. Here lie the true roots of a nation's life; here is the field for the cultivation of that noble patriotism, which, delighting in home, is yet free from Chauvinism, and by its tolerance and catholicity introduces the very element which insular Englishmen can least afford to dispense with. And the road to the study of Literature leads through the study of Language. A nation's language is the highest emblem and the best guarantee of the continuance of its national life. The first object of a foreign conqueror's aversion is the people's speech; no wonder, then, that all continental nations not only make Language and Literature compulsory, but they group the other studies round these; as all roads lead to Rome, so do all their studies converge on Language and Literature; Speech, Reading, Writing, Grammar and Composition, are regarded and treated as component parts of one organic whole; but, strange to say, England, the country whose language is the finest of all living languages, whose literature holds an all but

---

* Literature, but not in the Code's sense, where it merely means "learning by heart 100 lines of poetry."

undisputed pre-eminence, makes only Reading compulsory, and leaves it to the teacher's "speculative" judgment to decide whether Language and Grammar shall be taught or not; but the poor teacher is urged and bound to decide on the vulgar principle of the most "prudent venture," from the grant-earning point of view. As in the Universities the studies are divided into Classics and Mathematics, so in elementary schools the studies should be divided into Language and Arithmetic. Earnestly do I hope therefore that, in the new Code promised us by the Department, Language will occupy a position at least equal with that of Arithmetic.

For the better understanding of these foreign Standards, I proceed to explain two terms of frequent occurrence, viz. "Intuition" and "Denk-und Sprechübungen" = Practice in Thinking and Speaking.

On Intuition.

The word Intuition, derived from the Latin *intueor*, is a very imperfect English translation of the French *intuition*, which again is intended for an equivalent of the German Anschauung. The French also translate Anschauungsunterricht by "l'enseignement basé sur l'aspect," or teaching based on conceptions and ideas rendered visible. Now such intuitive teaching is of two kinds, according as it serves as a means or as an end. The former, the Germans call den Unterricht veranschaulichen; the latter, Anschauungsunterricht. An example or two of each will best explain the difference between them. If on a rainy day the teacher took his pupils to some piece of ground gently inclined, and showed them how the tiniest runlets of rain-water combined to form a larger water-course, how several of these again combined to form one still larger, and so on; if then he told the little ones to remember what they had seen, and afterwards, drawing it on the black-board, asked them to recognize and explain it, he would have made observation subservient to the end of explaining water-courses, maps, &c. Or, again, if he renders visible the double meaning of division by placing actual counters before his class, he has also caused the conception of the idea to be derived from the observation of actual things. "Realistic teaching" would in many cases not be a bad translation of the German phrase, "den Unterricht veranschaulichen."*

For a good example of Anschauungsunterricht, of the kind where it serves as an end, not as a mere means, I cannot do better than go to the admirable "Report on Belgian, German and Swiss Schools," made in 1865 by Monsieur Baudouin to the French Ministry of Education.† I find on p. 86 :

"L'enseignement simultané, l'enseignement basé sur l'aspect, comme disent les Allemands, occupe constamment l'intelligence des enfants et ne permet pas à leur attention de se relâcher."‡

Again, on p. 95 :
"*Enseignement par l'Aspect*, or *Teaching by Observation.*
"This method of teaching, employed in all German elementary

---

* In a course of "Lectures on Teaching," lately published, I find the following passage : "It is not an uncommon fault among Pestalozzian teachers to employ what are sometimes (*sic*) called intuitional methods long after they have served their purpose, and when the pupil is quite ready to deal intelligently with abstract rules." My own experience does not bear out this charge; Pestalozzians certainly do at *each stage* start from the Concrete, but they rise to the Abstract with all convenient speed. In speaking of Intuition thus disparagingly, both here and elsewhere, the lecturer is at variance with the leading Education Ministries of all Europe. Either Europe, then, is mistaken, or the learned lecturer.

† My thanks are due to the School Board for London for having kindly lent me this splendid volume.

‡ Mr. X. Y. Felkin, a member of an eminent Nottingham firm, who has resided many years in Saxony, and is a very competent judge, has just published a very able pamphlet, "Technical Schools in a Saxon Town," where on page 23 I find Anschauung enumerated amongst the subject of studies, and he says : "'Anschauung:' Teaching to observe, think and to reason is the foundation of all German teaching. It is given in the two lowest classes by itself (i.e. Intuition as an end), and then merged in the different subjects taught (i.e. Intuition as a means). It is the *most important of all kinds of instruction, and forms the child's mind, and develops his powers of observation.*" The italics are Mr. Felkin's.

schools, produces excellent results; it is simple, pleasant to the children, and as easy to use in large as in small schools; but it requires trained and earnest teachers, who are capable of carrying on a conversation enlivened by interesting details, who possess that knack of teaching which consists in making the children find out the answer instead of telling it them, who take the trouble to revive their own knowledge and to vary their studies so as not to weary the children by mere periodic repetitions.

"In spite of the length of the details already given, I will explain still further this method of teaching, and give an exact idea of it, by means of three examples of lessons adapted to the three classes of a large primary school.

"Lower Division. The teacher takes in his hand some common object, such as a ball, a cane, a cube, a hat, a book, &c., and, standing in front of the form nearest to his desk, he begins to talk with the children.

"He tells them the name of the object which he holds in his hand, its form, its colour, how and where it is made, what it is used for, &c. Then he asks questions of those children whom he considers the most advanced, and lastly he addresses the whole class, who answer together.

"First Division (of the lower class). The master is standing in front of one of the pictures hanging on the walls of the school-room; the picture represents, let us suppose, a dense forest. In the first half a number of animals are collected who all live in woods, but not necessarily in the same part of the world; in the second half a family of wood-cutters are returning, laden with faggots, to their home; and at a little distance there is a forester with a gun on his shoulder.

"*Teacher.* Tell me, Weber, what does this picture represent?

"*Pupil.* A forest.

"*T.* (*In an undertone*). Ah! this picture represents a forest; but how did you find that out?

"*P.* By the trees.

"*T.* Then, directly you see some trees, you say, There is a forest.

"*P.* No; there are gardens full of trees.

"*T.* What are those gardens called?

"*P.* Orchards.

"*T.* Ah! orchards? Why aren't they called forests?

"*P.* Because the trees in the orchards aren't of the same sort as those in the forest.

"*T.* What trees are usually found in an orchard?

"*P.* Apple-trees, pear-trees, cherry-trees, &c.

"*T.* And what sorts form forests?

"*P.* Oaks, firs, beeches, birches, &c.

"*T.* Which are those that you see on the left-hand side of the picture?

"*P.* These are oaks.

"*T.* Do you see nothing but oaks?

"*P.* I see some firs too. (The pupil points with his finger to the firs in the picture.)

"*T.* How else do you know that this wood is a forest, and not an orchard?

"*P.* By the animals: the animals which I see in this picture for the most part live only in forests.

"*T.* What animals do you see?

"*P.* A fox, some stags, some squirrels.

"*T.* By what do you know a stag?

"*P.* By his antlers.

"*T.* What are all these animals called?

"*P.* Quadrupeds.*

"*T.* Why quadrupeds?

"*P.* Because they have four feet.

"*T.* Are only quadrupeds found in the woods?

"*P.* Bipeds† are found there too.

"*T.* Tell me some.

"*P.* Birds.

"*T.* By what are birds known?

"*P.* By their wings and their feathers.

"*T.* But are all the parts of a bird covered with feathers?

"*P.* No, not its beak nor its feet.

"*T.* Is there anything else which shows that it is a forest?

"*P.* This man and woman (the child points to the wood-cutter and his wife).

"*T.* What are they carrying?

"*P.* Faggots of dry branches.

"*T.* Where have they collected them?

---

* This answer would in English seem too advanced for a child; but the German word Vierfüssler tells its own tale.

† The same remark holds of bipeds.

"*P.* In the forest.

"*T.* What do you see over there?

"*P.* A huntsman.

"*T.* Is it an ordinary huntsman, who hunts game in the field?

"*P.* No, I made a mistake; it's a game-keeper.

"*T.* What is he doing in the forest?

"*P.* He watches to prevent people taking away wood.

"*T.* Ah, he is there to prevent people taking wood; so no one has the right to gather wood in the forest?

"*P.* No, not without his leave.

"*T.* And he who does take some, what does he do?

"*P.* He steals.

"*T.* Has that man who is speaking to the keeper been stealing?

"*P.* No, that is a wood-cutter who has just cut some wood.

"*T.* Why do you think he is a wood-cutter?

"*P.* Because the wood which he is carrying on his shoulder has been cut and not broken, and, besides, because he is not afraid of speaking to the keeper.

"*T.* Well, then, now tell me all your reasons for concluding that this is a forest.

"*P.* First, because of the kind of trees; secondly, because of the sort of animals; thirdly, because of the dress of the keeper; and lastly, because of the wood which the man carries on his shoulder, and because he is talking friendlily with the forester.

"During this conversation, which can be adapted to a thousand different subjects, or enlarged, as we shall see, with very instructive details, all the pupils are on the watch, ready to answer themselves if their little schoolfellow makes a mistake or even hesitates. At the first slip they almost all hold up their hands, asking to be questioned, and showing an animation which proves the interest they take in the lesson, greater than would be expected in children eight or nine years old."

It is not necessary to quote the two lessons to the more advanced classes.

Such "Intuition lessons" form the starting-point of most branches of study in the Elementary School; gradually they become "intuitive lessons," till in the advanced classes the pupils having been trained into habits of clear thought with sharp outlines and clear statements of them, the teacher is safe in trusting to his pupils' powers of abstract thought. All this is meant by the phrase, "from the Concrete to the Abstract."

In these conversation classes, or Denk-und Sprechübungen, as the Germans call them, the children are made to speak in simple grammatical sentences, with correct pronunciation and distinct enunciation; and these habits of speech and thought, so formed, constitute the bases and starting-points of the subsequent lessons in Reading, Grammar, Syntax, Analysis and Logic. Even Geography, beginning as it does with Heimathkunde, knowledge of home, starts from conversations on objects and scenes personally observed either in the school or on excursions.

In concluding this Introduction, I cannot do better than quote M. Baudouin still further. On p. 233, he speaks thus of Leipzig and of Saxony:

"The town of Leipzig, always ready to indulge in the luxury of one school more, first gives aid to this new establishment,* and shortly after, if it prospers, adds it to the list of its numerous institutions of public instruction.

"Happy town, which, in the surging tide of commercial life and activity, always remembers that it is the native town of the great Leibnitz, and forgets how to count when the education of its children is in question!

"Happy country, Saxony! She has taken advantage of fifty years of peace conceded to her, first to teach her people, and then to develop her industry. Primary schools have been opened in all the smaller localities, and elementary knowledge has been sown broadcast over the land. The higher instruction, encouraged by Government, has advanced pari passu, and has made famous the schools of Meissen and of Grimma, the University of Leipzig, the Mining School of Freiberg, the Academy of Fine Arts of Dresden, &c. Thanks to the spread of knowledge and to the intelligence of the inhabitants, manufactures have attained a high degree of perfection, and certain branches of industry advantageously compete with England† in the principal markets of Europe."

* A new secondary school.

† This fact has grown in truth and in importance since 1865. Mr. Felkin says, p. 65: "Nottingham, which has hitherto had the supremacy, now com-

On p. 489, M. Baudouin says:

"In Switzerland every one busies himself with Popular Education; every one is interested in its progress. The honorary duties of local managers are respected and coveted; the ministers of religion encourage teachers and families; and the State guarantees the existence of teachers, and keeps public instruction up to a high level by constant watchfulness over the schools and the observance of the law. It is now a well-established fact that Switzerland, at present so calm and so prosperous, only arrived at this state of things during the last thirty years by having incessantly striven to improve, to perfect, her system of public instruction, adopting the excellent innovations of that people,* who, if you please, are somewhat viewy (rêveur, Schwärmer), but who have grown more reasonable in proportion as they have been better taught; always ready to speak, to write and to sing, but slow to pull up paving-stones and make revolutions, which benefit nobody."

And M. Baudouin's concluding words (p. 497) shall also be mine:

"Some persons have an interest in keeping things as they are, and trouble themselves very little about the common good; it is useless to try to convince them. Others, though full of the best intentions, doubt the efficacy of the remedy proposed; to them I say: 'Germany plains that Chemnitz is taking the trade away, owing to the cheapness of Saxon labour. This no doubt is a main cause, but is it the only one? Cheap labour may enable the Chemnitzers to get the trade, but cheap labour alone, with the existing outlook, will not enable them to keep it; for without trained intelligence and technical knowledge on the part of the workmen, and enterprize among the manufacturers, it would soon revert back again . . . . if labour is cheap in Saxony, and the trade there has its Technical School educating young men, how necessary is it that the people of Nottingham, fighting against these odds, should strain every nerve and omit no means to hold their own!" Again, on p. 60: "*The large manufacturers of Bradford, Huddersfield, Salford, &c., send their sons here, because there are no institutions of the same kind in England.*" Again, on p. 70, foot-note, "The first lace-machine has left Nottingham for Plauen in Saxony. More are to follow. How many will there be in Saxony in ten years' time I leave the reader to surmise. Twenty years or more ago this very same experiment was tried with lace-frames, and failed, as technical knowledge was insufficient amongst the workmen. Now it is sufficient, and the success is assured."

† The Germans.

and Switzerland are not so very far. Do as I have done. Give up all foregone conclusions, visit those countries, where all the measures taken have led to progress and to prosperity ; see and decide.'

"As for myself, I shall not consider my time nor my labour lost, if I have contributed, in ever so small a degree, to destroy those ideas of universal superiority which our national self-esteem is pleased secretly to foster, to inspire in us the desire of regaining in Education that prominent position which in other things we have for a long time been so reluctant to yield to others, and to hasten on the School Reform demanded by modern progress, and rendered urgent and indispensable by the new conditions of society."

STANDARDS FOR ARITHMETIC.

"When Plato introduces Arithmetic as the first of the Sciences which are to be employed in this mental discipline, he adds (vii. § 8) that it must be not mere common Arithmetic, but a science which leads to speculative truths* seen by Intuition (τῇ νοήσει αὐτῇ), not an Arithmetic which is studied for the sake of buying and selling, as among tradesmen and shopkeepers, but for the sake of pure and real science."—*Whewell's Republic of Plato*, p. 304.

AARGAU.

First Class (in summer 3, in winter 4 hours per week).
Computation up to 20:
    (*a*) Counting of concrete objects up to 10.
    (*b*) Symbolizing of these numbers by strokes.†
    (*c*) Practice in Addition and Subtraction, using the abacus or other apparatus.
    (*d*) Notation up to 20.
    (*e*) Application of the symbols + − × ÷ =
    (*f*) First steps in Multiplication and Division.

Second Class (in summer 3, in winter 4 hours per week).
Computation up to 100:
    (*a*) Counting of concrete objects up to 100, by gradual addition of units, introducing the notion of "tens."
    (*b*) Numeration and Notation of numbers up to 100.
    (*c*) Addition and Subtraction of numbers 20—100.

* ἐπὶ θέαν τῆς τῶν ἀριθμῶν φύσεως.
† See Pestalozzi's Table of Unity.—The COMPILER.

(d) Mental Arithmetic, pure and applied.
(e) The most indispensable acquaintance with Swiss coins and with the commonest weights and measures.
(f) Solution of easy Rule of Three problems solely by means of Multiplication and Division.

Third Class (in summer 2, in winter 4 hours per week).
Computation up to 1000:
(a) Extension of the circle of numbers up to 1000.
(b) Notation of units, tens, hundreds and thousands.
(c) Frequent dictation by the teacher of numbers with three or four digits to be placed under one another.
(d) Oral practice in Multiplication and Division, and thorough learning of the Multiplication-table.
(e) *Extended acquaintance with coins, weights and measures.
(f) Mental Arithmetic, with applications.
(g) Resolution and Reduction in writing.
(h) Written Arithmetic: the Four Rules, but multiplier and divisor to be of one digit only.

Fourth Class (in summer 2, in winter 4 hours per week).
Computation up to 100,000:
(a) Numeration and Notation of numbers with six digits.
(b) Dictation, Addition and Subtraction.
(c) Multiplication and Division, with multipliers and divisors respectively of one, two and three digits; applied problems.
(d) Simple problems on Interest, Averages and Partnerships, mentally and in writing.

Fifth Class (in summer 2, in winter 4 hours per week).
Computation in numbers beyond 100,000:

---

* Contrast this early and graduated study of the simple Swiss coins, weights and measures, with our Standards, where a knowledge of the coins is not required till the third Standard, and the study of our long and perplexing weights and measures constitutes a portion of the fourth Standard.

AARGAU.

(a)*Multiplication and Division, with multipliers and divisors respectively of several digits. The usual artifices for contracted operations.
(b) Continuation of problems on Interest, Averages and Partnerships, worked mentally and in writing.
(c) First stages in Fractions, based on "intuition."†
(d) Complete knowledge of Swiss coins, weights and measures.
(e) Rule of Three applied.
(f) Areas.

Sixth Class (hours as in fifth).
Vulgar Fractions:
(a) Complete knowledge of Vulgar Fractions.
(b) Deduction of principles of calculation with Vulgar Fractions.
(c) Rule of Three, Interest and Partnerships, requiring Vulgar Fractions.
(d) Areas and Volumes.

Seventh Class (in summer 3, in winter 4 hours per week).
Computation with Decimal Fractions, rendered visible by means of Vulgar Fractions:
(a) Explanation of the nature of Decimal Fractions and their notation.
(b) The Four Rules applied to Decimals.
(c) Interconversion of Decimals and Vulgar Fractions.
(d) Application of Decimals to Per-centages and to commercial Arithmetic (Waarenrechnung).

---

* Such gradual extension of the pupils' horizon in ever-widening circles, continental pedagogues call "concentric teaching."

† "Intuition" is here, and all through this work, taken in the strict, literal sense of "beholding," from the Latin "intueor," *I behold*. It is difficult to find an exact English equivalent for the German Veranschaulichung and Anschauung: Intuition is bad, but Inspection seems to me worse.

28   *ARITHMETIC.*

Eighth Class (hours as in seventh Class).
- (a) Rule of Three, simple and compound, with Vulgar and with Decimal Fractions.
- (b) Difficult problems on Interest.
- (c) Profit and Loss, Partnerships, &c., requiring fractions.
- (d) Per-centages and commercial Arithmetic.
- (e) Book-keeping by single entry.

ALSACE-LORRAINE.

First School Year (Practice in the numbers 1 to 20).

1. Practice (Uebung). Value of numbers 1 to 10 taught intuitively by number-pictures and by counting.

2. Practice. Addition of pairs of numbers of one digit each, taught first on the abacus and next by number-pictures. (N.B. The sum of the two numbers must not exceed 10; this practice must be continued also without apparatus or objects *till absolute mastery is gained*). Frequent applications of these problems to practical affairs. Introduction into these problems of common weights, measures and coins, in so far as they are within the horizon of the children's experience.

3. Practice. Subtraction of pairs of numbers of one digit rendered visible on the abacus and by many other means. Exercise and application to follow intuition.

4. Practice. Numbers 10 to 20 rendered visible, followed by Addition and Subtraction of numbers 1 to 20.

5. Practice. Addition of two numbers of one digit whose sum exceeds 10. (N.B. What was said under Practice 2 about intuition, exercise and application, applies also to Practice 5; in these results also *absolute mastery* must be acquired.)

6. Practice. Subtraction of numbers of one digit from numbers under 20. Method as in Practice 3.

7. Practice. Resolution into factors of the numbers 1 to 20, to be rendered visible on abacus and other apparatus. This practice leads to:

 (a) The Multiplication-table of numbers 1 to 20. (For method, see Practice 11.)

 (b) Division of the products of the Multiplication-table by an Abstract Divisor, or Division in the sense of Distribution. This Practice is the converse of the last. In the former, the factors are given and the product is to be found; in the latter, the product is given and the factors are to be found. .... The children gain the necessary insight only if such distribution is *rendered visible.*

 (c) Measurement of the products of the Multiplication-table, or Division in the sense of Being Contained. .... Such measurement being rendered visible on the abacus by showing, for example, how many times 3 is contained in 6, 9, 12, 15 and 18.

Appendix: In the seven Practices above enumerated, figures are to be employed only *after the numbers have been rendered visible.* .... The children will be led to indicate the numbers on the slate by lines, dots or crosses; they will imitate the number-pictures mentioned in Practice 1; e.g. ⁝⁝ The children are also to learn soon to make practical application of what they have learnt, by setting forth in figures the processes followed in Mental Arithmetic.

Second School Year.

8. Practice. The genesis of the numbers 20 to 100 rendered visible. Practice in counting backwards and forwards. Notation and Numeration 20 to 100.

9. Practice. Addition of a number of one digit to one of two digits. It is imperative that this important Practice be taught on the abacus. The number to be added must be so decomposed as first to complement the next higher multiple of 10. After the

children have sufficiently realised this process, they are to be practised *in the formation of series*. (N.B. This Practice offers a wide field for written exercises. . . . . The first few terms to be supplied to the children either on the black-board or from the Arithmetic books in use in the school.*)

10. Practice. Subtraction of a number of one digit from one of two digits. Here, too, intuition is absolutely indispensable, especially in the passage from one multiple of 10 to another, such as is necessary in $52-7$. The process must be repeated and rendered visible on very many examples. The N.B. of Practice 9 is also here applicable.†

11. Practice. The Multiplication-table. It is self-evident that the teacher must drill the pupils into a ready knowledge of the Multiplication-table (geübt), but it cannot be sufficiently insisted upon that the children must first have obtained a *complete insight* into the meaning before they are subjected to this drill. Therefore the problems of the Multiplication-table must be rendered visible on the abacus, so that the children may understand the meaning of such phrases as 3 times 8.

12. Practice. Division of the products of the Multiplication-table. On the method of teaching this Division, both in the sense of "distribution" and of "being contained," see Practice 7.

Third and Fourth School Years.

The 12 Practices above enumerated constitute the basis of the whole elementary instruction in Arithmetic; and unless they have been mastered, all further progress is uncertain and retarded. As all the subsequent studies are only a continuation of the structure on the bases indicated, it is unnecessary to describe the subsequent stages in such detail. It is sufficient to lay stress on the following principles:

---

* Kentenich's Praktische Rechenschule or J. Menzel's Rechenfiebel.

† The translator supposes that in Practice 9 the pupils are required to write down *ascending*, and in Practice 10 *descending* series.

I. Children must understand the value of numbers before they are allowed to deal with them. Where intuition is no longer possible, it is indispensable to analyse the numbers into tens, hundreds, thousands, and so on. Thus is obtained the *insight into the structure of our Scale of Notation*, which is indispensable in written Arithmetic (slate Arithmetic).

II. The principal task in an elementary School is, and always will be, to practise the children in *Mental Arithmetic;* they should at least be able rapidly and with accuracy to solve the following problems :

(*a*) Addition and Subtraction of numbers with two digits.

(*b*) Multiplication and Division of a number of two digits by a number of one digit.

In teaching, the following points must steadily be kept in view :

1. In Mental Arithmetic, the teacher must endeavour to prevent the pupils imagining the quantities *written*. In Mental Arithmetic, the mere symbols must step into the background.

2. It is not sufficient to practise the children in finding the solution; they must also be able to exhibit the process of reasoning in logical and grammatical speech, and if required in writing.

3. In verbal solution, rapidity must not be neglected.

4. Examples applied to the affairs of life, such as the children can make immediate use of, should not be neglected. A little attention to the claims which life makes upon the skill of the children, will make it easy for the teacher to hit the right thing, and to revert to it by frequent repetition. Thus drill in the products 12, 15, 16, 20, 24, 25, 30, 50 and 60, cannot be sufficiently recommended.

5. It is desirable that in Mental Arithmetic the teacher should follow the sequence of some book, such as the Mental Arithmetic book by Menzel.

III. In written Arithmetic, with larger numbers, i.e. using figures, the following points are to be observed :

ARITHMETIC.

1. Avoid working with *very large numbers*. The zeal of children easily flags when they have to manipulate large numbers; moreover, such examples, especially of multiplication with very large factors,* have no practical value.

2. Every process must first be thoroughly explained to prevent work which is purely mechanical.†

3. In written Arithmetic, the teacher must insist on the greatest neatness and accuracy. Care must be taken that the figures are clear, placed in proper columns, and the necessary lines be ruled. Calculation on paper is permitted only in the senior classes.

4. Written Arithmetic tasks are also to be given for homework, &c. &c.

The three or four last School Years.

The first four years having treated of Integral Arithmetic, concrete and abstract, there are yet two branches to be disposed of:

1. Fractional Arithmetic (Vulgar and Decimal Fractions).
2. Commercial Arithmetic.

---

* What would the Herr Ober-Präsident von Elsasz-Lothringen say to one of his Inspectors if he plucked children because they failed to multiply 7096 by 7096 ? This problem, whose product exceeds 49 millions, was lately given by one of H. M. Inspectors to children of the Second Standard, who are supposed not to know numbers beyond 100,000.

† Contrast with the following: "We now proceed to work multiplication of two or more figures. Having multiplied by the units' figure, show that in commencing to multiply by the tens' figure the first figure of the product is placed under the tens' figure of the line just obtained, or that it is perpendicularly under the figure by which you are multiplying, which, as it holds good, whatever power the multiplier may be, I try to impress well. (*But how if, instead of giving the problem in the shape* $\frac{47682}{365}$, *it were given* 47682×365?) Here it is necessary to cause each figure to be placed in its proper position, so that there may be no difficulty or error in adding the lines together. I do not here go much into the subtleties (to a child) of the decimal system of notation, for which there was a mania some twenty years ago, it being then strongly advocated that every step in the practical working of the simple rules even, should be accompanied *pari passu* with an exhaustive explanation of its theory." This is from a series of articles on "How I teach Arithmetic," by a teacher who has been highly praised for his method by one of our foremost Inspectors.

A.—Fractional Arithmetic.

Arithmetic of Vulgar Fractions forms a principal subject of Mental Arithmetic. Practical life requires great readiness in dealing with halves, thirds, quarters, &c.; moreover, we must not lose sight of the fact that Arithmetic of *Vulgar* Fractions forms the basis of Arithmetic with *Decimal* Fractions.

For Arithmetic with Vulgar Fractions, stress is to be laid on the following points:

1. Although the pupils must be acquainted with fractional nomenclature both from the affairs of life and from calculations in the earlier stages, still it is necessary, before beginning fractional Arithmetic, to render fractional values visible in all their details. Thus only, and not by definitions, do children get correct notions of Fractions.

2. Exercises should be principally given on such fractions as $\frac{a}{2}, \frac{a}{3}, \frac{a}{4}, \frac{a}{5}, \frac{a}{6}, \frac{a}{8}, \frac{a}{10}, \frac{a}{12}, \frac{a}{24}, \frac{a}{25}, \frac{a}{50}$. Though other fractions may be introduced, drill should be chiefly concentrated on these fractions. Large quantities, especially in mixed numbers, are to be avoided.

3. The following practices are specially important.
   (*a*) Conversion of concrete fractions into concrete integers (e.g. $\frac{3}{4}$ franc = 15 sous).
   (*b*) Interconversion of integers, mixed numbers and improper fractions.
   (*c*) Reduction of fractions to lowest terms.
   (*d*) Multiplication of a fraction by an integer.
   (*e*) Division of a fraction by an integer.

To these may be added, according to circumstances: expansion of fractions, reduction to a common denominator, addition and subtraction.

Decimal Fractions follow Vulgar Fractions in such a manner that every rule in Decimals finds its justification and demonstration in the corresponding rule for Vulgar Fractions. . . . Let the teacher guard against all working by routine: let him *explain every process* before applying it. . . . .

B.—Commercial Arithmetic.

The solution of problems of Rule of Three, Interest, &c., is effected by a proper combination of Multiplication and Division both in Mental and in Written Arithmetic. No child ought to leave school who cannot solve the commonest and simplest problems of prices, areas, &c., *without using a Ready Reckoner*. . . . . Therefore children are to be taught the *Unitary Method*, with frequent explanations and oral solutions often repeated.

AUSTRIA.

General Aim: Accuracy and skill in oral and in written solution of arithmetical problems of civil life. Elements of Book-keeping by single entry.

First School Year. The Four Rules applied to numbers 1 to 20 mentally and in writing. Coins, weights and measures, in so far as their sub-multiples can be expressed by tenths. Written Arithmetic must correspond with Mental Arithmetic in form and in sequence of ideas.

Second School Year. The Four Rules applied to numbers 1 to 100 mentally and in writing. Coins, weights and measures, in so far as their sub-multiples can be expressed by hundredths. Elements of Fractions.

Third School Year. Expansion of the circle of numbers to thousands and thousandths.* The Four Rules, with Integers and Decimals. Unitary Method. Mental Arithmetic.

Fourth School Year. The Four Rules, with Integers and Decimals. Calculation with numbers of different denominations

---

* It is to be remembered that the use of the Metric System gives to continental teachers an especial advantage at this stage.

and with vulgar fractions of common occurrence. Mental Arithmetic.

Fifth and Sixth School Years. Divisibility of Numbers. Conversion of Vulgar Fractions into Decimals, and vice versâ. Conversion of numbers of different denominations into Vulgar and Decimal Fractions, and vice versâ. The Four Rules in Integers and Fractions, concrete and abstract. The most common artifices for contracted operations. Mental Arithmetic.

Seventh and Eighth School Years. Extraction of the Square Root. Ratios and Proportion. Discount, Partnerships, Chain Rule. Principles of Book-keeping by single entry. Mental Arithmetic.

The girls are to be specially instructed in Household Accounts.

Hours of study : First Standard, six half-hours per week ; subsequent Standards, boys 4 hours, girls 3 hours per week.

CITY OF BALE.

PRIMARY SCHOOL FOR GIRLS.

First Class. Calculation in numbers 1 to 20. Analysis of numbers.

Second Class. Calculation in numbers 1 to 100.
 1. Addition and Subtraction of the fundamental numbers (i.e. 1 to 9 inclusive) orally and in writing.
 2. Multiplication-table up to 10 × 10 (in sequence).

Third Class. Expansion of circle of numbers up to 1000 and 10,000. Practice in the Four Rules.
 A.—Mental Arithmetic.
 1. Addition and Subtraction of numbers with one and two digits within 1 to 100.
  Examples : 64 + 8, 40 + 30, 50 + 23, 33 + 60, 59 + 36, and so on.
  97 − 9, 90 − 60, 60 − 47, 74 − 50, &c.

36 *ARITHMETIC.*

    2. Multiplication-table up to 10 × 10.
    3. Resolution into factors of the products of the Multiplication-table.
       Examples: $24 = 3 \times 8, 4 \times 6, 6 \times 4, 8 \times 3$;
                    $36 = 4 \times 9, 6 \times 6, 9 \times 4$, &c.
    4. Division (Distribution, and Being Contained).
       Examples: 2 in 18, 3 in 12, 5 in 30, 6 in 54, 9 in 72, &c.
         $\frac{1}{2}$ of 6, $\frac{1}{4}$ of 24, $\frac{1}{8}$ of 40, $\frac{1}{10}$ of 90, &c.

B.—Written Arithmetic.

Up to Multiplication by multiplier of one digit.

Optional. Division by divisor with one digit.

Numeration of numbers with three and four digits.

Fourth Class. Expansion of numbers up to 100,000 and 1,000,000. Practice of the Four Rules.

  A.—Mental Arithmetic.
    1. Addition and Subtraction of numbers of one, two and three digits from 100 to 1000.
       Examples: $70 + 50, 80 + 36, 72 + 70, 284 + 9, 370 + 50$,
               $720 + 65, 413 + 70, 460 + 330$, &c.
              $200 - 40, 400 - 120, 813 - 8, 430 - 80$,
              $590 - 33, 672 - 60, 980 - 420$, &c.
    2. Multiplication.
       Examples: $5 \times 20, 7 \times 80, 6 \times 40, 5 \times 15, 6 \times 27$, &c.
    3. Division (Distribution and Being Contained, with and without remainder).
       Examples: 2 in 24, 8 in 56, 7 in 42, 3 in 26, 7 in 50, 9 in 70.
         $\frac{1}{2}$ of 24, $\frac{1}{3}$ of 48, $\frac{1}{5}$ of 80, $\frac{1}{6}$ of 102, $\frac{1}{7}$ of 105
         $\frac{1}{8}$ of 120, &c.

Applied problems.

Examples of greater difficulty may be written on the blackboard.

B.—Written Arithmetic.

  The Four Rules up to Multiplication by multiplier with

three digits, and Division with divisor with two digits. Numeration and Notation of numbers with five and six digits.

Applied examples: acquaintance with the coins, weights and measures in common use.

BAVARIA.
I. *Junior Classes.*
A.—Mental Arithmetic.
1. The idea of number to be given by intuition.
2. Counting 1 to 10 forwards and backwards; then 10 to 100.
3. Easy examples of Addition and Subtraction to form basis of intuitive Multiplication-table.

B.—Written Arithmetic.
1. Knowledge of figures.
2. Numeration and notation up to 100.
3. Easy concrete problems in Addition and Subtraction.

C.—Knowledge of the usual weights and measures.

II. *Intermediate Classes.*
A.—Mental Arithmetic.
1. Counting and skipping from 100 to 1000 forwards and backwards.
2. Practice in Subtraction and Multiplication.
3. Easy artifices.

B.—Written Arithmetic.
1. Numeration and notation of the above numbers.
2. Simple problems in the Four Rules, concrete and abstract.

C.—Continuation of weights and measures.

III. *Senior Classes.*
A.—Mental Arithmetic.
1. Exercise in larger numbers.
2. The Four Rules continued, simple and compound.

3. Systematic arrangement of the most important artifices, with rationale for the same.

B.—Written Arithmetic.
1. Numeration and notation to millions.
2. Practical problems in the Four Rules.
3. Unitary Method and simple Fractions.
4. Weights and measures.

BELGIUM.

Lower Primary Schools.

First Stage* (for children from 6 to 8 years).

A.—Arithmetic, mental, intuitive and in figures.

1. Numeration. The Four Rules combined in the following order: (*a*) numbers 1 to 10; (*b*) numbers 1 to 20; (*c*) numbers 1 to 100.

2. Special study of the Multiplication-table, and its application to Division of numbers 10 to 100 by a number not exceeding 10.

3. Knowledge of tenths and hundredths of Units. The Four Rules on these magnitudes.

4. Knowledge of Fractions whose denominator does not exceed 10; formation, denomination and notation.

5. Small problems having a bearing on the affairs of daily life. Exercise of invention, or problems proposed by the pupils themselves.

Care must be taken to have recourse to visible processes representing the magnitudes wherever that is possible.

---

* Each stage occupies two years. Belgium had no Standards till 1880. Finding this arrangement very hurtful to the cause of Education, Mr. Vanhumbeck, the Education Minister of Belgium, published by decree, 20th July, 1880, the present Standards. Being a *new* administrative act, it was found desirable to leave some latitude to teachers and inspectors in several minor points.

B.—The Metric System. This need not be given here, as unfortunately for us we are still wedded to our mediæval systems of weights and measures.

Second Stage (for children from 8 to 10 years).

A.—Numeration.

Numeration and dictation of Integers and of Decimal fractions. Formation, denomination and notation of Vulgar Fractions whose denominator does not exceed 20.

B.—Arithmetic, mental and intuitive.

The Four Rules. Explanation by familiar examples of the object and use of each Rule.

First Series. Numbers formed (*a*) of tens and units; (*b*) of units and tenths; (*c*) of tenths and hundredths.
1. Addition.
2. Subtraction.
3. Multiplication (*a*) by a number of one digit; (*b*) by 10; (*c*) by a multiple of 10; (*d*) by a number formed of tens and units.
4. Division (*a*) by a number of one digit; (*b*) by 10.

Second Series. Numbers formed (*a*) of hundreds, tens and units; (*b*) decimal fractions not comprising magnitudes less than thousandths.
1. Addition.
2. Subtraction.
3. Multiplication (*a*) by a number of one digit; (*b*) by 10, 100, 1000; (*c*) by a multiple of 10; (*d*) by a number formed of tens and units. Examples of multiplication by 5, 9, 11, 15, 19, 25, 50, 99.
4. Division (*a*) by a number of one digit; (*b*) by 10, 100, 1000; (*c*) by a number consisting of tens and units.

Vulgar Fractions (denominator not exceeding 20).

Conversion of mixed numbers into fractions, and vice versâ. Addition and subtraction of fractions having the same denominator. Multiplication and Division of fractions by an integer less than 10. (N.B. The demonstrations to be rendered visible as much as possible.)

C.—Written Arithmetic.

The science and the art of the Four Rules applied to Integers and to Decimal Fractions.

Vulgar Fractions. Conversion and Four Rules within the limits indicated above under Mental Arithmetic.

D.—Application of Mental and Written Arithmetic in the progressive sequence of this course.

Numerous problems borrowed from the affairs of life, from trades, agriculture, &c. Some easy problems on Simple Interest. Exercise of invention, or problems proposed by the pupils themselves.

E.—Metric System (continued and extended).

Third Stage (for children from 10 to 12 years old).

A.—Mental Arithmetic.

1. Numerous exercises on the Four Rules applied to integers and decimals. Principal artifices for rapid calculation.

2. Vulgar Fractions. Conversion of fractions into others of equal value. Reduction of two or more fractions to a common denominator. Addition and Subtraction, Multiplication and Division:

(*a*) Of a fraction by an integer, and vice versâ.
(*b*) Of a fraction by a fraction.
(*c*) Of a fraction by a mixed number, and vice versâ.
(*d*) Of a mixed number by a mixed number. Applications.
(N.B. The demonstrations to be rendered visible.)

B.—Arithmetic.

1. Rationale of numeration of integers and decimals.

2. Very elementary theory of the Four Rules on integers. Find quotient of two integers within $\cdot 1$, $\cdot 01$, $\cdot 001$, approximately.

3. Criteria of divisibility by 2 and 5, by 4 and 25, by 8 and 125, by 9 and 3, by 11. Test of accuracy in Multiplication and Division by casting out nines.

4. Definition of prime numbers and of numbers prime to each other.

Application (without proof) to division by factors of the principle that *If a number is divisible by two or more numbers prime to each other, it is divisible by their product.*

Resolution of numbers into prime factors (without demonstration). G.C.M. of two numbers, and L.C.M. of two or more numbers.

5. Elementary theory of Vulgar Fractions: genesis and definition; Numeration; fundamental properties; simplification of fractions; reduction of fractions to their simplest form; fundamental operations; conversion of Vulgar Fractions into Decimals.

6. The Unitary Method applied to:
   (a) Rule of Three.
   (b) Simple Interest.
   (c) Profit and Loss per cent.
   (d) True Discount.
   (e) Proportional parts and Partnership.
   (f) Averages.

7. Numerous examples bearing on the affairs of life, and on trades, domestic economy, rural economy, &c. Exercises of invention, or problems proposed by the pupils themselves.

C.—The Metric System.

Recapitulation of the Metric System. Application of measures of surface to the calculation of the area of the parallelogram, the lozenge, the trapezium and the circle. Application of the measures of volume to the calculation of the volume of the prism, the cylindre, the pyramid, the cone and the sphere. Relationship subsisting between the weights and measures of volume and of capacity.

Upper Primary Schools.

A.—Mental Arithmetic.

Solution of problems mentally.

B.—Arithmetic.

1. Criteria of divisibility by 2 and 5, by 4 and 25, by 8 and 125, by 9 and 3, by 11. Test of accuracy in Multiplication and Division by casting out nines.

2. Recapitulation of instruction given in the preceding course on resolution of numbers into prime factors on G.C.M. and L.C.M. of two or more numbers.

3. Recapitulation, with further development, of the theory of Vulgar Fractions. Notions on the origin and nature of a recurring decimal. Reduction of a given recurring decimal to a vulgar fraction.

4. Definition of Ratio. Definition of Proportion (by means of quotient*). Product of extremes equals product of means. Given three terms, to find the fourth. Direct and inverse Proportion.

5. Unitary Method. Solution of new problems on Simple Interest, true Discount, proportional parts and Partnerships. Use of Ready Reckoner for calculation of Compound Interest. Usual problems on Stocks and Shares, mixtures and alligation.

6. Practical rules on extraction of Square and Cube Roots. Application. Finding a mean proportional between two given numbers.

7. Notions on Equality and Equations. Numerical Equations of the first degree with one or two unknown quantities. Problems.

C.—The Metric System.

Problems applying the relationship subsisting between the different measures.

Specific Gravity explained. Use of specific gravity.

---

* Meaning of course that the magnitudes are assumed to be commensurable.

Relative value of coins of equal weight, and relative weights of equal value.

Of the division of the Circle into degrees, minutes and seconds. Of the divisions of Time. Calculation of numbers of the different denominations that these lead to. Problems on measuring surface and volume of geometric magnitudes.

CANTON OF GENEVA.

First Stage.

Intuitive teaching. Numeration and notation of numbers up to 20. Mental Arithmetic up to 10, according to Part I. Ducotterd and Teacher's Guide.

Second Stage.

Numeration, Addition and Subtraction of numbers up to 1000 (not inclusive). Subtraction to be worked by borrowing,* the minuend not containing a nought. Mental Arithmetic up to 20. Exercises on Part II. Ducotterd, up to p. 11 inclusive, edition 1878.

Third Stage.

Numeration of numbers under 10,000. Addition and Subtraction of these numbers. Multiplication by numbers with two digits. Multiplication by 10 and by 100. Proofs. Mental Arithmetic. Practice on numbers up to 100. Elementary problems consisting only of three small numbers (Exercises of Ducotterd, from p. 12 of Part II. to the end and the first five pages of Part III.; second series of problems by Duchamp).

Fourth Stage.

Multiplication of integers under 100,000. Division by numbers of two digits. Mental Arithmetic. Proofs, exercises, easy problems (Part III. Ducotterd; third series, Duchamp).

* "Emprunt," meaning *not* paying back to subtrahend; the common method of borrowing from minuend and paying back to subtrahend is called "compensation" (see Neuchatel).

Fifth Stage.

Numeration and notation of any numbers whatsoever. Summary of rationale of the Four Rules applied to integers. Numeration of Decimal Fractions. The Four Rules applied to Decimals. The Metric System. Mental Arithmetic exercises; easy practical problems (Part IV. Ducotterd, and the first 431 numbers of Part V., fourth series, Duchamp).

Sixth Stage.

Relation of the Metric units to the commonest units of the old weights and measures. Vulgar Fractions. Conversion of Vulgar Fractions into Decimals, and vice versâ. Reduction of numbers of different denominations to fractions, and vice versâ. Unitary Method. Rationale of processes. Mental Arithmetic (end of Ducotterd, Part V. and Part VI.; fifth series of Duchamp).

HAMBURG.*

Class I.—A knowledge of Numbers from 1 to 10, and from 10 to 20, with easy Mental Arithmetic involving these numbers. Also some knowledge of the numbers up to 100.

Class II.—The Arithmetic of Numbers up to 100. Introduction to the numbers from 100 to 1000.

Class III.—The elementary rules of Arithmetic, both mentally and written. An elementary knowledge of fractions.

Class IV.—Vulgar and Decimal Fractions, and the Solution of easy Questions requiring a knowledge of fractions.

Class V.—A more thorough knowledge of all the earlier steps in Arithmetic, with calculation of remainders. Interest. Profit and Loss. Bills of Parcels. Money. Calculation of Exchanges.

Class VI.—More thorough knowledge of the work prescribed

---

* Taken from the "Report on Schools in Germany and Switzerland," by George B. Davis, Clerk to the Birmingham School Board.

for Class III. The first four rules of Algebra. Easy equations of the first stage. Extraction of the square root.

Class VII.—More difficult problems involving a knowledge of all the rules of Arithmetic, particular attention being paid to the business calculations required in merchants' offices and in industrial life. In Algebra, simple equations containing one or more unknown quantities, easy quadratic equations, involution and evolution.

[The aim of the course in Arithmetic and Algebra is to give the pupils a clear insight into the laws of numbers, and their relations to one another, and to enable them to solve skilfully and accurately all the ordinary arithmetical questions that occur in practical life. Also, to make them quick in mental arithmetic.]

ITALY.

Preliminary Instruction. In the elementary schools, Arithmetic must be taught in a manner altogether practical. Let the master abstain from giving demonstrations which would not be understood at that tender age. Let him limit himself to impressing well on the minds of the pupils the definitions and the working of the Four Rules, and to see that they are worked expeditiously and without hesitation.

When the teacher proposes concrete problems, the questions proposed must be most simple, so that the pupils may readily perceive the connection between the requirements of the problem and the particular operations required for its solution.

To teach what little is requisite of the notation of vulgar fractions, let the teacher begin by explaining with precision the meaning of the fractions $\frac{1}{2}, \frac{1}{3}, \frac{1}{4}, \frac{1}{5}$, &c., and let him subsequently cause the pupils to construct tables of the multiples of these fractions.

From such tables will naturally follow the notions of proper and improper fractions and of mixed numbers, the idea of composite numbers, and the rule for converting an improper fraction into a mixed number, and vice versâ.

In teaching the Rule of Three, let the teacher's principal aim be to communicate to his pupils a sure criterion for distinguishing the cases to which this rule applies.

First Year. Mental Exercise in Addition and Subtraction. Reading and writing of Arabic figures.

Second Year. Numeration and notation of numbers with several digits. Addition and Subtraction of Integers. Multiplication by Integers.

Third Year. Division of Integers. The Four Rules with Decimals. Definition and free-hand drawing of the most important geometrical figures. The Metric System. Solution of simple problems with concrete numbers.

Fourth Year. Meaning of a fraction. Proper and inproper fractions and mixed numbers. Interconversion of fractions. Reduction of an improper fraction to a mixed number, and vice versâ. Conversion of a vulgar fraction to a decimal. Rule of Three by Unitary Method. Applications.

MUHLHAUSEN.

The instruction in Arithmetic begins with counting concrete objects, then proceeds to the manipulation of abstract numbers till they are fully mastered. Advancing gradually and the circle of numbers expanding, larger and larger numbers are successively treated in all possible ways. From this follow the Standards for the several classes:

First Class. Addition and Subtraction of numbers 1 to 20.

Second Class. The Four Rules applied to numbers 1 to 100. The Multiplication-table up to 10 × 10 taught by multiplication and division.

Third Class. Recapitulation of the Multiplication-table. Numeration. The Four Rules applied to larger integers.

Fourth Class. The extended Multiplication-table up to 10 × 20, so as to multiply and divide with ease by all numbers up to 20 in one line. Calculation in integers of different denominations. Arithmetic applied to Time.

Fifth Class. The Metric System rendered visible by apparatus and drawing, and practised in decimal and vulgar fractions.

Sixth Class. Continuation of decimal and vulgar fractions specially applied to Rule of Three. Interest, Discount, Alligation, Partnership, &c.

Seventh Class. Continued practice of the several rules. The elements of Geometry. Square and Cube Root. A few hours are devoted to elementary instruction in Book-keeping.

NEUCHATEL.

In Arithmetic the application of the proverb "Little and well" is of prime necessity. We shall therefore proceed gradually and without leaps, leaving no gaps. We shall not begin a new rule before the preceding one is well understood. By the side of the mechanical labour of calculation purely abstract, the master will take care to devote a large part of his time to operations on concrete numbers, otherwise the child, failing to perceive the utility of the operations taught him, and only seeing masses of figures to add, subtract, multiply and divide, will infallibly be disgusted with Arithmetic. The problems which the child will have to solve will be at first short, simple, practical, and within his scope. Later on, gradually advancing, the calculations will expand *pari passu* with the child's development. An excellent method it is to lead the child in the path of discovery, and make him invent examples on the rules of Arithmetic he is studying. (Arithmetical Composition). . . .

ARITHMETIC.

In all the Standards the teacher will frequently demand that the working of problems be fully reasoned out orally, and occasionally this shall be done in writing also. Verification is to be made regularly in every Standard. . . .

Recapitulation is the mother of study. Thus at each stage and after each promotion, the teacher will consider it his duty to recapitulate with his new student the field traversed in the class immediately below. In every Standard there will be numerous exercises in Mental Arithmetic.

Lower Grade.

First Year. 1. Mental Arithmetic. Counting from 1 to 100 forwards and backwards. Which number precedes and follows a given number? Even numbers from 2 to 100 forwards and backwards. The same with the odd numbers. Skipping tens up to 100, commencing first with 0, then with 1, 2, 3, 4, &c.

The Four Rules applied to numbers 1 to 20 worked mentally. Easy problems of practical use. Frequent use of the abacus. Duration of lesson, a quarter to half an hour.

2. Theoretical Arithmetic, writing figures. Numeration 1 to 100. Numerous exercises on the relative value of units, tens and hundreds.

3. Practical Arithmetic. Addition, Subtraction (by equal additions*). Numerous and varied problems.

Second Year. 1. Mental Arithmetic. Numbers up to 100. Lessons and exercises on the multiples and submultiples of the different units of time, weights, lengths, &c.; on the usual prices of foods, beverages, materials, &c. Find $\frac{1}{2}$ $\frac{1}{3}$ $\frac{1}{4}$ $\frac{1}{5}$ of a number. Practical problems.

2. Theoretical Arithmetic. The same exercises as in the first year from 1 to 1000. Decomposition of numbers. Theory of the four simple Rules. Arithmetical symbols. Sum, Difference, Multiplicand, Multiplier, Product, Dividend, Divisor, Quotient.

---

* "Compensation;" cf. Geneva.

Different applications of each of the Four Rules illustrated also by decimals of a franc.

3. Practical Arithmetic. Recapitulation of Addition and Subtraction. Multiplication and Division (the divisor not to exceed 999). Verification of Division by Multiplication, and vice versâ. Numerous problems.

Intermediate Grade.

First Year. 1. Mental Arithmetic up to 200. Same exercises as last year. Multiplication and Division by 5, 10, 50, 100.

2. Theoretical Arithmetic. The Decimal System. Numerous exercises on moving the decimal point. Elements of the Metric System, &c.

3. Practical Arithmetic. The Four Rules decimally, with numerous problems to illustrate the theory.

Second Year. 1. Mental Arithmetic to 500. Problems for practice.

2. Theoretical Arithmetic. The Metric System continued.

3. Practical Arithmetic. Problems to practise the Metric System.

Upper Grade.

First Year. 1. Mental Arithmetic up to 1000. Problems for practice on Vulgar Fractions. Compound numbers (units of Time) and the Metric System.

2. Theoretical Arithmetic. Complete theory of the Metric System. Divisibility of numbers. Theory of Vulgar Fractions. Prime Numbers, Factors, Divisors, Multiples, Common Denominator. Properties of Fractions.

3. Practical Arithmetic. Recapitulation of the Metric System. Vulgar Fractions.

4. Book-keeping. Debit and Credit. Cash-book. Notes and Invoices.

Second Year. 1. Mental Arithmetic on the Metric System, Interest, Discount, &c.

2. *Theoretical Arithmetic.* Recapitulation of the Metric System. Conversion of Vulgar Fractions to Decimals, and vice versâ. Unitary Method.

3. *Practical Arithmetic.* Application of the Unitary Method to the Rule of Three, simple and compound; to Interest, Discount, Partnership, Mixtures, &c. Various problems.

4. *Book-keeping.* Inventory, Journal, Ledger.

PRUSSIA.

1. AIM AND METHOD.

The study of Arithmetic is to enable pupils to make independently, rapidly and accurately, both mentally and in writing, those calculations which occur in the affairs of life, in integers as well as in fractions. The instruction is to be given at every stage in such a manner that the student shall be exercised in logical thought and precise expression. Mere mechanical calculation is to be strictly avoided. Children must always gain insight into the reasons of the processes.

At every stage, abstract and applied calculations are worked together. In the senior class, applied problems assume a prominent position.

The problems of applied Arithmetic must bear principally on current coins, weights and measures, and must be taken from the life and experience of the pupils. For this reason, large numbers with many digits are to be avoided.

In beginning a new Rule, Mental Arithmetic must precede Written Arithmetic.

2. STANDARDS.

Sixth Class (4 hours). Counting, Addition, Subtraction and breaking-up of a number into two parts, applied to all numbers up to 10.

Fifth Class (4 hours). Gradual expansion of the circle of

numbers up to 100. Addition and Subtraction of numbers of one digit. Multiplication and Division in both senses (of Distribution and Being Contained) to be thoroughly practised upon the products of the Multiplication-table. Applied problems.

Fourth Class (4 hours). Gradual expansion of the circle of numbers up to 1000. Mental Arithmetic with numbers of two digits (principally under 200) on the Four Rules. Coins, weights and measures. Applied problems to consist of simple calculations of prices, wages and consumption.

Third Class. Recapitulation of the work of the first three years, with increased difficulties (mentally). The Four Rules on paper. As soon as the children have mastered the normal methods, they are to be practised in the application of artifices of contraction, both mentally and on paper.

Second Class (4 hours). The Four Rules, mentally and on paper, with numbers of any magnitude. Easy Fractions, Vulgar and Decimal, Rule of Three.

First Class. Recapitulation of the work of the preceding year, with more difficult Vulgar and Decimal Fractions. The Four Rules in Decimals, conversion of Vulgar Fractions into Decimals, Decimal system of weights and measures.

Proportion, direct, inverse and compound, Chain Rule, Percentages, Profit and Loss, Discount, Partnership, Alligation, Areas and Volumes, and Evolution.

SAXONY.

The Arithmetic lessons are to enable the pupils to make all calculations occurring in the affairs of life promptly and independently.

Teaching is to be realistic and progressive (entwickelnd); special attention being devoted to oral and written solutions of practical problems with small numbers.

All mere mechanical work to be sternly banished from the outstart; clear perception of the problems and of the rules required for their solution, verbal explanation with distinct utterance, and independent discovery by the pupils of the most important Rules, are to be steadily aimed at.

All Arithmetic in the elementary schools is to be a training in thinking; for thus only can be attained the necessary emancipation from mere symbols learnt by heart and used mechanically, thus only can really be gained that self-reliance in computation which is required for practical life.

The first four years of school are devoted to the study of the Four Rules on the numbers 1 to 10, 1 to 100, 1 to 1000, both simple and compound, concrete and abstract; numbers beyond 1000 are exceptionally admissible in Written Arithmetic, if full mastery has been attained in the Four Rules on the lower numbers; in Mental Arithmetic they are wholly forbidden. At the same time, the children must be taught German coins, weights and measures, elements of Vulgar and Decimal Fractions, and the Unitary Method.

In the last four years, the Four Rules are recapitulated, expanded and finished; Fractions, vulgar and decimal, are taught thoroughly, and applied to Commercial Arithmetic. Rule of Three sums are to be taught solely by the Unitary Method.

Oral and Written Arithmetic to be taught simultaneously.

At each stage Mental Arithmetic must precede and lead up to Written Arithmetic.

In Written Arithmetic, neatness and accuracy of execution must be insisted upon.

CANTON DE VAUD.

[Considerable latitude is left to the teacher's initiative with respect to the number of years to be devoted to each of the three grades, as this must to a great degree depend on local circumstances, on school accommodation, &c.; but on the whole it is expected that the lowest grade will take two years; the intermediate grade, two to three years; and the highest grade, three to four years. In an extreme case, then, a child would require nine years, i.e. from 6 to 15, to go through the whole curriculum.—THE COMPILER.]

Lower Grade.

1. Numeration up to 10. The Four Rules on these ten numbers. The exercises to be worked first mentally on visible objects and then in writing.

2. Numeration up to 100. Skipping forwards and backwards by 2, 3, 4, 5, first from 1 to 20, next from 1 to 50, and lastly up to 100. Numerous exercises rendered visible and worked mentally on the relative values of units, tens and hundreds. Multiplication and Division up to 30. Problems worked mentally and in writing.

3. Continuation of the above exercises. Skipping forwards and backwards by 6, 7, 8, 9, 10, up to 100. Multiplication and Division mentally and in writing, with multiplier and divisor respectively of one digit, and multiplicand and dividend of two digits at most. Some of the simplest and most useful Measures.

Intermediate Grade.

1. Numeration of Integers up to 100. Fractions rendered visible. Mental Arithmetic on Integers and on simple Fractions.

Written Arithmetic. The Four Rules, simple, on Integers up to 1000 and on some easy Fractions. The multiplier and divisor to consist of no more than two digits.

Money; measures of length and of capacity; weights; and divisions of time.

2. Mental Arithmetic continued. Recapitulation and theoretic study of the Four Rules, dwelling principally on Division. Verification of Division by Multiplication. Criteria of divisibility by 2, 3, 4 and 5.

Notation of Decimal Fractions, connecting them with numeration of Integers. Shifting of the decimal point. Reduction of Decimals to a common denominator.

The Four Rules applied to Integers and Decimals. Numerous problems with applications to measures of length and of surface.

Upper Grade.

Mental Arithmetic. Problems of graduated difficulty on the different kinds of Rule of Three, Interest, &c., on Integers and Fractions.

Rule of Three, Simple and Compound Interest, Partnership and other Rules connected with Rule of Three, Averages. Numerous problems taken as much as possible from ordinary life.

The Metric System and its relations to Swiss weights and measures. Numerous problems. Recapitulation and amplification of the theory of Decimals. Conversion of Vulgar Fractions to Decimals, and vice versâ. Terminating and recurring Decimals. Book-keeping by single entry. Waste-book, Journal, Ledger and Letter-copying.

CITY OF ZURICH.

ELEMENTARY SCHOOL.

First Standard.

Notions of the numbers 1 to 10 rendered visible on concrete objects by gradual addition and subtraction of units, and corresponding representation of the same on the black-board by marking and wiping out of lines or dots till absolutely clear conception is attained. . . . . . . Expansion up to 100, gradually adding units and introducing the notion of tens, and skipping by the intervals 1 to 5 up to 100. Finally, Notation up to 100, and repetition by means of these symbols.

Second Standard.

Skipping by 6 to 10 up to 100. Expansion up to 200 by adding new units and collecting them into tens and rendering visible the hundred itself. Addition and Subtraction of numbers of one digit, of multiples of ten, of numbers of two digits; transition to Multiplication and Division, by REPEATED addition and subtraction of the same numbers 1 to 10.

Third Standard.

Practice of Multiplication and Division by numbers of one digit, with multiplicand and dividend respectively up to 100 till absolute mastery and readiness is attained. Thorough study of the Multiplication-table. Extension up to 1000. Addition and Subtraction of numbers of one, two and three digits. Multiplication and Division of these by numbers of one digit.

In all three Classes constant repetition in concrete numbers and application of what has been learnt to very simple problems.

Realschule* (Intermediate Classes).
Fourth Standard.

I. Expansion to higher numbers of more digits. Theoretic study of the decimal scale of notation. Practice in Multiplication and Division up to 10,000, by numbers of two digits, and easy practice with compound numbers. Frequent oral and written solution of applied problems, taken as much as possible from the children's experience. The problems are to be in numbers that can be rendered visible, requiring processes of reasoning, where the chain of reasoning is easily surveyed.

II. Elements of Geometry rendered visible, &c.

Fifth Standard.

I. Arithmetic. Repetition of earlier practices till absolute mastery is obtained in Addition, Subtraction, Multiplication and Division of larger numbers, both simple and compound. First notion of Fractions. Addition and Subtraction of Fractions with like denominators. Multiplication and Division of Fractions by Integers, but only by altering the numerator. Applied problems

* A term used here in an exceptional sense.

as in the fourth Class, inclusive of simple combinations of the Four Rules in one problem and in the simple Unitary Method.

II. Geometry . . . .

Sixth Standard.

I. Arithmetic. Multiplication and Division of Fractions by Integers by altering the denominator. Interconversion of Fractions. Reduction to least common denominator. Addition and Subtraction of Fractions with different denominators, and Multiplication and Division of Integers by Fractions. Applied problems as in fourth and fifth Classes.

II. Geometry . . . .

COMPLEMENTARY SCHOOLS.

Seventh Standard.

I. Arithmetic. Finish Vulgar Fractions. Solution of numerous problems by Unitary Method, simple and compound, taken from practical life. Contracted operations.

II. Geometry . . . .

Eighth Standard.

I. Arithmetic. Fundamental notions of Decimals and their notation. Conversion of Decimals into Vulgar Fractions, and vice versâ. Addition and Subtraction of Decimals. Applied problems as in the previous class, with increased difficulty.

II. Geometry . . . .

Ninth Standard.

I. Arithmetic. The Four Rules in Decimals, applied problems; Book-keeping.

II. Geometry . . . .

STANDARDS FOR LANGUAGE.

AARGAU.

First and Second Classes.
(In summer 9, in winter 10 hours.)

1. Intuition. Examination and correct perception of well-known objects in the school, home and neighbourhood, with the view of cultivating the child's powers of observing objects, their properties and uses. Correct nomenclature and description of the objects observed, in simple sentences, so as to attain to a power of expression commensurate with the stage of intellectual development arrived at by the child.

2. Writing and Reading. *First Class.* Preliminary practice of the ear, of the organs of speech, of the eye and of the hand. Thorough study of the Primer (Fibel).

Second Class. (a) Reading of descriptions and narratives with very distinct enunciation.

(b) Practice in speaking both by describing the objects treated of in the Intuitive lessons, and by reproducing the descriptions and narratives of the Reading lesson.

(c) Easy lessons on Composition, based on the models furnished by the Reading lesson.

(d) Written exercises; transcription, and solution of problems given in the Reading-book; dictation of words and phrases.

(e) Learning by heart and recitation.

Third and Fourth Classes.
(In summer 7, in winter 12 hours.)

Third Class. (a) Intuition. Examination of and conversation on plants and animals, as well as on natural phenomena and human employments according to the seasons. Local topography.

(b) Reading with correct intonation and enunciation, and with greater ease and readiness.

(c) Practice in Syntax and in the grouping of phrases.

(d) Reproduction of the matter read in local patois and in grammatical speech (Mundart und Schriftsprache).

(e) Learning by heart and recitation.

(f) Writing. Transcription; reproduction in writing of a precedent oral reproduction. Descriptions; narratives; solution of grammatical problems; writing from memory and from dictation, for the study of both Spelling and Punctuation.

Fourth Class. (a) Reading, with explanation, of the first four sections of Part III. of the First Lesson and Reading-book. Study of Roman characters.

(b) Practice in oral reproduction of the matter read. Descriptions, comparisons and imitations.

(c) Learning by heart and recitation.

(d) Written practice; transcription; writing from memory pieces learnt by heart, and reproduction in writing of what has already been reproduced orally.

(e) Grammar. Rules and practice on Parts of Speech. Syntax and Orthography according to Part V. of the Lesson and Reading-book.

Fifth and Sixth Classes.
(In summer 5, in winter 7 hours.)

(a) Reading with still greater ease and more correct intonation.

(b) Oral practice: reproduction of the matter read; paraphrase of poems, narratives, descriptions and comparisons; matter and plan of composition indicated by the teacher.

(c) Recitation from memory. In the Sixth Class, explanation of prevalent inaccuracies of expression.

(d) Reproduction in writing of what has previously been reproduced orally; transcription from memory; descriptions and comparisons previously discussed. First steps in Letter-writing.

(e) Grammar. Rules and practice in Syntax, Orthography and Word-building, according to Part V. of the Reading-book.

SEVENTH AND EIGHTH CLASSES.
(In summer 3, in winter 7 hours.)

(a) Reading with ease, and with elegance of intonation and expression.

(b) Oral practice in reproduction of a narrative or a description; explanations and analogies; condensation of the Reading lesson. Close and free imitation of the style.

(c) Recitation of classical pieces learnt by heart.

(d) Reproduction in writing of matter previously read or of themes previously discussed. Letters and business letters.

(e) Grammar and Analysis on the basis of the corresponding section in the Reading-book.

ALSACE-LORRAINE.

The aim of the lessons in German is to enable the pupil readily and accurately to express his ideas orally and in writing. But it must be constantly kept in view that the child should acquire an adequate amount of knowledge in such a thorough manner as to retain it, and that the subject-matter read in the Reading-book should influence and stimulate his character, so as to give him culture, and excite in him the love of God and of man, patriotism and reverence and loyalty to the Emperor, to the law and the rulers of the land.*

* Passages such as these show the impossibility of any one nation adopting the regulations of another; still they offer food for reflection.

SUBJECTS AND METHODS OF INSTRUCTION.

(a) *Lower Stage.*

Exercises in Speaking constitute one of the chief means of developing the child's knowledge of his mother-tongue. In the first weeks they serve as an introduction to Reading; later on, their object is to enlarge the child's range of observation and to develop his power of expression. Fit subjects of conversation are natural objects, or good pictures of them within the domain of the child's mental horizon; also proverbs, apophthegms and little poems.

The early Reading lessons, which constitute one of the most important tasks of this stage, aim at imparting to the child some skill in reading easy pieces printed both in German and in Roman characters. The teacher must carefully guard against the error of practising at this stage merely the so-called mechanical reading, to the neglect of reading with intelligence and expression. Even at this stage it is indispensable to apply the rules of universal validity concerning correct pronunciation and enunciation of words and phrases.

Writing is taught in connection with Reading according to the method of the Primer (Fibel) used in the school. Spelling is better taught through the eye than through the ear, so that attentive reading affords the best foundation for this study; written practice in Spelling is to commence with words spelt phonetically, so that the word can be analyzed into its sounds,* where sounds and their symbols are in perfect accord. After the children have learnt also the names† of the letters, they can be

---

* This is always possible in German and in Italian; in English and in French, the maxim, "dans la lecture, les véritables éléments des mots sont les syllabes," is most generally valid. Let the reader try to break up "mon" into *three* sounds, or, breaking up hat and hut into three sounds each, differentiate between *a* and *u* clearly enough for a child to be able to appreciate the two sounds; to say nothing of such words as grove, love, &c.

† The *names* of the letters are only taught after their *functions* are well known.—THE COMPILER.

made to spell and write down words and sentences out of the Primer, attention being drawn to any divergence between sound and spelling, to long and short sounds, and to the correct use of capitals.

Oral teaching by heart of apophthegms and little poems, after they have been fully explained by the teacher.

(b) Intermediate Stage.

The lessons in Language are in this Stage, as well as in the next Stage above, based on the Reading-book used in the school.

The principles laid down in the Lower Stage apply also here, but greater attention is to be devoted to reading with expression and to modulate the voice so as to suit the matter read.

The selection of the pieces of both prose and verse is to be made with a view of offering suitable mental exercise, and furnishing pieces to be learnt by heart. (The selection of poems to include the songs required in the Singing lessons.) . . . .

Practice in Spelling to extend to transcription of whole paragraphs out of the Reading-book. Smaller sentences are to be written from memory, the teacher having first pronounced them to the class, who repeat them after him; the most difficult words in the sentence being discussed and spelt orally. Punctuation is taught not only by strict observance of the pauses in speaking and reading, but also by explanation of the significance of these pauses.

(c) Upper Stage:

The principles laid down in the last Stage are valid also here; but at this Stage a special aim is to train the pupils in oral and written reproduction of the matter read, the rendition being sometimes very literal, at other times free.

Dictation. Whole sentences retaining their logical connection shall constitute the unit of Dictation, thus enabling the pupils correctly to appreciate the several members of the sentence, and to adapt the punctuation accordingly.

Composition. Subject-matter to be within the range of the child's mental horizon. It can be selected from the other branches of study, such as Geography, Naturkunde, &c. (Realien).

Letters and Commercial Correspondence, &c., first according to some model given, and afterwards free, the principal points merely having been indicated.

The pieces to be learnt by heart are patriotic songs and poems commemorating events and traditions of the history of the country, the teacher having previously fully explained them.

In the Intermediate and Upper Stages a special hour a week is set aside for the study of Orthography and Grammar, the rules being made clear and studied (Veranschaulichung und Uebung) in a thoroughly practical manner, according to a book which will shortly appear.

In conclusion, let it be well understood that instruction in Language is not to be confined to the Reading and Grammar lessons specially devoted to that purpose; on the contrary, every lesson is to be a lesson in Language in this sense, that the teacher insists, with utmost care and persistency, on purity of pronunciation, on completeness of utterance and correctness of expression.

AUSTRIA.

Aim: Clear understanding of statements made in the mother-tongue; fluent and correct expression, orally and in writing. Reading with expression written and printed matter.

First School Year.

Preliminary exercises in speaking, and inspection of objects taken from the child's surroundings; practice of sounds and their symbols, both written and printed; slow reading, with correct pronunciation, paying attention to the division of words into syllables; discussion of the matter read; graduated transcription from the Reading-book. Easy poems learnt by heart.

Second School Year.

(*a*) Reading. Reading with correct pronunciation, paying attention to the punctuation. Explanation of both the matter and the expression of the text. Answering of questions on the matter read. Suitable pieces learnt by heart.

(*b*) Grammar. Practice in Orthography, paying attention to long and short sounds, to division of words into syllables, and to the use of capitals. The simple sentence. Nouns, Adjectives and Verbs. The three principal Tenses. Graduated transcription from the Reading-book.

Third School Year.

(*a*) Reading. As in the last stage, but with increased demands.

(*b*) Grammar. Practice in Orthography, as in the last stage. The simple sentence. Inflections. Word-building by derivation and composition. Government of cases by Verbs and Prepositions. Written practice as in the last stage, and written reproduction of pieces from the Reading-book according to questions set.

Fourth School Year.

(*a*) Fluent and intelligent reading; explanation of matter and of diction. Reproduction of subject read. Practice in the various ways of putting a subject. Learning by heart.

(*b*) Grammar. Practice in Orthography, introducing words of like sound and different spellings. The enlarged simple sentence. Distinction between simple and complex sentences. Inflections, especially of Noun and Verb. Word-building by derivation and composition. Government of cases by Verbs and Prepositions. Written reproduction of short pieces read; easy correspondence.

Fifth and Sixth School Years.

(*a*) Reading as in the last stage, with increased demands.

(*b*) Grammar. Orthography, introducing words of foreign origin. The contracted and the complex sentence. Word-building. Kinship of words. Government of cases. Reproduction of short pieces read. Composition of narratives, descriptions, letters.

Seventh and Eighth School Years.

(a) Reading with fluency and expression both printed and written matter. Word and intonation to be carefully attended to. Rendition of contents and sequence of ideas in a piece read. Explanation of the subject-matter read and of the expression. Learning by heart of suitable pieces.

(b) Grammar. Orthography with words of foreign origin. The complex sentence. Punctuation. Conjunction. Summary of Inflections and of the principles of Word-building. Kinship of words. Government of cases. Narratives, paraphrase of poetry, descriptions, correspondence and business letters, &c.

CITY OF BALE.
Primary School for Girls.

First Class.

1. Intuition lessons, i.e. examination and naming of concrete objects of the child's surroundings. The actual objects to be exhibited wherever possible; where this is not possible, in good pictures.

2. Statement of the qualities and uses of the objects examined.

3. Correct transcription of German print out of the Primer (Fibel).

4. Explanation of sense and expression.

5. Analysis of words into syllables and sounds.

Second Class.

1. Continuation of the Intuition lessons and their application to speaking and writing, gradually enlarging the sphere of the Intuition in the same manner as in the previous Class (partly in connection with the Reading lessons and partly upon free selection).

2. Explanation of sense and expression in connection with the Reading lesson.

3. Analysis of words into syllables and letters. Spelling.

4. Correct transcription upon the slate of short pieces from German print.

5. Dictation and learning by heart.

6. Singular and Plural.

Third Class.

1. Continuation of the Intuition lessons in connection with practice in speaking and writing, with constant enlargement of the sphere of Intuition in the same manner as in the two preceding Classes.

2. Explanation of sense and expression in connection with the Reading lesson.

3. Transcription (on slate or on paper) of short pieces read, indicating the division into syllables. Transcription of stanzas of poetry in lines of verse.

4. Copying from memory of phrases and short pieces learnt by heart.

5. Dictation of Reading pieces previously prepared.

6. Word-building according to the exercises given in the Reading-book.

7. Elementary knowledge of Noun, Article, Adjective and Verb.

8. Optional: Some knowledge of the three principal Tenses of the Verb.

Fourth Class.

1. Explanation of sense and expression in connection with the Reading lesson.

2. Transcription of short pieces learnt by heart.

3. Dictation of pieces previously prepared.

4. Elementary knowledge of the Personal Pronouns and of the Numerals.

5. Some knowledge of the declension of Nouns with the Article (and with the Adjective).

6. Knowledge of the four tenses, viz. Present, Imperfect, Perfect and Future. Practice in interconversion of persons, numbers and tenses, by the aid of examples given.

7. Knowledge of the most important members of a sentence (Subject and Predicate).

8. Interrogative, Optative and Imperative Moods.

9. Short descriptions of objects inspected and discussed. Composition. Easy tales.

In all the four Classes, appropriate apophthegms, extracts and songs, are to be learnt by heart, and fixed in the memory by frequent repetition.

BAVARIA.

I. *Junior Classes.*

A.—Speaking.
1. Children pronounce words and short phrases after the teacher.
2. Correction of pronunciation, intonation and enunciation.
3. Practice in connected speech, by narrating short tales taken from the child's life.

B.—Reading.
1. Study of the letters.
2. Slow reading with intelligence and expression.

C.—Writing. The fundamental strokes of small Cursiv-schrift letters advancing to single words.

D.—Grammar. Practical knowledge of the most important parts of speech, and first steps in Declensions and Conjugations.

II. *Intermediate Classes.*

A.—Speaking.
1. Children continue to pronounce after the teacher longer phrases, apophthegms, proverbs, &c.

2. Practice in oral delivery, children repeating what they have heard or read.
B.—Reading. Reading with ease, intelligence and expression, different kinds of print and type.
C.—Writing. Calligraphy from copies set.
D.—Grammar.
   1. Complete knowledge of all the parts of speech, with all the Declensions and Conjugations.
   2. Application of this knowledge in writing short themes.
E.—Orthography.
   1. Principles of Orthography.
   2. Analysis of audible words into sounds, &c.
   3. Derivation of words.
   4. Knowledge of commonest abbreviations, &c.
   5. Use of capitals.
   6. Words of like sound and different spelling.

III. *Senior Classes.*

A.—Speaking.
   1. Continuation of practice in oral delivery of narratives and descriptions.
   2. Continued study of correct pronunciation and of purity of expression.
B.—Reading. Reading with ease, intelligence and expression, different kinds of print and type.
C.—Writing. Calligraphy; perfectly free, without ruled lines or copy set.
D. Grammar.
   1. The anomalies of the language. Principal characteristics of a good style.
   2. Composition of short descriptions, narratives, reports, attestations, receipts, business and other letters, &c., selected so as to serve for suitable illustration of the laws of Grammar learnt.

E.—Orthography.
1. Application of the laws of Orthography in suitable themes and compositions.
2. Continued study of words of like sound and different meaning, and the correct use of punctuation and other signs.

BELGIUM.

LOWER PRIMARY SCHOOLS (see p. 38).

First Stage.
A.—Writing......
B.—Reading.
1. Combinations of sounds selected for reading and writing (written characters); during the first months, of words and short phrases giving some useful notion, being interesting at the same time, and not presenting any irregularity in spelling or pronunciation.
2. Knowledge of printed characters. Exercise in Reading.
3. Graduated practice of the most important irregularities, the knowledge of which is indispensable to fluent reading. "Liaison" of the words, as "vous-avez," "allons-enfants," "il est-arrivé." Punctuation.
4. First exercises in fluent reading. Conversation on the subject-matter read.
5. Expressive recitation of short pieces previously explained.
N. B. Local accent to be steadily combatted from the earliest exercises. Children to be taught pure pronunciation, and speech well articulated and sufficiently expressive. Extirpate (*sic*) the sing-song tone of the school.
C.—Spelling.
1. Dictation to practise the combinations taught. Oral decomposition of these combinations.

2. Formation of words and of short phrases by means of the elements taught.

3. Short pieces of dictation, taken mostly from the Reading-book.

4. Written reproduction from memory of one or more phrases, and afterwards of graduated extracts (morceaux) previously recited with expression.

D.—Mother-tongue.

I. Practice in Speaking (Exercises de Langage, being evidently a translation of the German "Sprech-übungen"). These exercises, which will bear chiefly on the objects to be found within the child's own sphere of observation, do not constitute a separate branch of study. It is nevertheless considered profitable at the outstart to hold special conversations on persons and things of the school and of the home. With this exception, it is necessary as soon as possible to connect the practical study of language and the various exercises presented by it with the discussion of natural objects, of moral recitations, of the reading lessons, of geometrical forms, and of the first notions of geography and history.

During the first months of the course, the teacher is forced not only to evoke ideas in the child's mind, but even to express them almost wholly himself. Gradually, as the intellectual horizon of the children grows larger and their vocabulary more ample, efforts must be made to lead them to express their sensations, observations and reflections, in simple, correct and complete phrases, well pronounced and accented.

II. Reproductions. Short reproduction in simple phraseology of the subject of the lessons (elementary notions of Natural Science, Geography, &c.).

III. Spelling: usual. The first lessons in Spelling advance pari passu with Reading and Writing.

IV. First notions of Grammar taught in an exclusively practical manner.

French.

1. Nouns and Articles. Gender, Number: principal rules for forming the plural.
2. The qualifying Adjective. General rules for forming the feminine and the plural.
3. The Verb. The three principal tenses.
4. The Pronoun. General idea of it.

Flemish.

1. Noun and Article. Number of Nouns.
2. The Adjective.
3. The Verb. The three principal tenses.
4. General notion of the Pronoun.

German.

1. The Noun and the Article. Gender, singular and plural, and Umlaut (as Bruder Brüder).
2. The Adjective.
3. The Verb. The three principal tenses.
4. General notion of the Pronoun.

Oral exercises in conjugations and in the formation of complete phrases; in the use of the commonest tenses of Auxiliary Verbs and of Verbs of frequent occurrence.

Exercises of application. Exercises of invention (the children being encouraged to compose statements and simple phrases).

Second Stage.

A.—Reading.

Subjects of a simple kind; recitations and moral precepts, fables and poems; extracts bearing on the lessons on Natural Science and useful knowledge.

Conversation on the subject-matter read; short explanation of the meanings of words and of the sequence of ideas. Free (oral) reproduction of the subject-matter of the Reading lesson. Reading of an extract. Once a week the children give account of what they have read at home. Expressive recitation of a piece previously explained.

B.—Mother-tongue.

I. Exercises in Speaking. These exercises are in connection with the lessons on Natural Science, Geography, History, &c., which are to be utilized for giving practical lessons in the formation of sentences by following a progressive sequence.

II. Reproduction, simple and graduated.
- (a) Description of objects taken from elementary notions on Natural Science.
- (b) Short analogies and comparisons.
- (c) Familiar letters.
- (d) Oral and written reproduction of a little moral tale or historical event related by the teacher.
- (e) Rendition of account of lessons, and of things read.
- (f) Commercial and professional Composition. Notes, memoranda, invoices, receipts and bills of lading.

III. Spelling: usual.
- (a) Examination of the spelling of the Reading lesson. Spelling from memory of words selected. Various remarks. Dictation of short paragraphs from the Reading-book previously discussed. Written reproduction from memory of extracts previously recited with expression.
- (b) Dictation of graduated short pieces. Explanation of ideas, of the meaning of the words, and of the spelling.

IV. Very simple Grammatical notions.

French.

1. Nouns, Articles, Adjectives, qualifying and determining, Pronouns and Verbs.

2. Distinction of parts of sentence, viz. Subject, Verb and Attribute.

3. The Noun. Common, Proper and Compound Nouns. Principal rules for forming the plural of Common Nouns. Complement of the Noun.

4. The Article. Elision and contraction.

5. The qualifying Adjective. Formation of the feminine and of the plural. Complement of the qualifying Adjective.

6. The Pronoun. Concords.

7. The Verb. Subject and Complement. Persons of the Verb. Principal Tenses. First idea of Moods. General rules of agreement between Verb and Subject. Conjugation (principally oral) of regular and irregular Verbs taught in complete phrases. Transitive and intransitive Verbs, active and passive voice.

8. General rules of agreement of the past Participle.

9. Recognition of words not subject to inflections.

Flemish.

1. Nouns, Articles, Adjectives, Numerals, Pronouns and Verbs.

2. The simple sentence: Subject, Predicate, Copula. Determination of the Subject and Predicate.

3. Noun and Article. Plural of Nouns. The four Cases. Inflection.

4. Adjectives. Inflection. Degrees of Comparison.

5. Verb. Persons of the Verb. Principal tenses. Moods. Conjugation of Auxiliaries (taught in connected sentences), of weak Verbs, and of the strong Verbs of most common occurrence. Transitive and intransitive Verbs. Active and passive voice.

6. Qualifying words. Practical knowledge.

German.

1. Nouns, Articles, Adjectives, Pronouns and Verbs.

2. The simple sentence: Subject, Predicate, Copula. Determination of the Subject and the Predicate.

3. Noun and Article. The four Cases. Inflection.

4. The Adjective. Inflection and Comparison.

5. Verb. Persons of the Verb. Principal tenses. Moods.

Conjugation (taught in connected sentences) of Auxiliary Verbs, of weak Verbs, and of strong Verbs of most common occurrence. Transitive and intransitive Verbs. Active and passive voice.

6. Prepositions and Adverbs. Practical knowledge.

Applications. Grammatical explanation of pieces previously read and discussed, so as to understand the ideas. Very simple analysis of the parts of the sentence and of speech.

Graduated grammatical exercises on subjects both useful and interesting. Exercises of invention.

V. Exercises on the derivation and composition of words. These notions shall be given along with the study of the piece read in the Reading lesson, giving attention to spelling and to grammar.

Roots, compound words, derived words; prefixes, suffixes, terminations; kinship of words.

C.—Writing. . . . . .

Third Stage.

A.—Expressive Reading.

Literary subjects, in prose and in verse, suitable for practical teaching of moral obligations.* Subjects to serve as complement to the intuitive lessons on Natural Science and useful knowledge.

Explanation of the subject-matter read, both as to its sense and its grammatical form. Reading with expression. Recitation with expression of pieces previously explained.

N.B. The teacher will say a few words on each of the most famous authors.

B.—Mother-tongue.

I. Exercises in Elocution. The aim of these exercises is to habituate the pupils to express their own ideas with clearness

---

* The reader will have observed the stress frequently laid by Belgium on the teaching of moral duties and obligations. In connection with this, it is worth remembering that Austria, Germany, France and Switzerland, include Religion in the curriculum of their Elementary Schools; Belgium excludes it.

and precision on subjects chosen from the sphere of their own experience.

The subjects to be selected are very various, and are connected principally with the explanations accompanying the Reading lessons, with the reproductions, which are all the better for having previously been treated vivâ voce, and with lessons in History, Natural Sciences, &c.

It is not to be forgotten that the aim is not to make the pupils recite from memory, but that they should well express their own observations, thoughts and sentiments.

II. Graduated reproductions.

 (*a*) Description of common objects. Descriptions taken from the study of elementary Natural Science. Comparisons.
 (*b*) Familiar correspondence.
 (*c*) Narratives.
 (*d*) Summary of lessons. Rendering an account of some walk, tour or excursion.
 (*e*) Commercial and professional correspondence, &c. Notes, memoranda, invoices, receipts, certificates, contracts, bills of exchange, &c. &c.

III. Grammatical notions.

French.

1. Recapitulation, by means of Reading lessons, and Dictation of the principal rules taught in the preceding stage.

2. Various kinds of sentences. Conjunctions which serve to connect them. Grammatical Analysis and Syntax reduced to their essential elements.

3. Rules of Punctuation.

4. Plural of proper and compound Nouns.

5. Use and omission of the Article.

6. Agreement of the Adjective.

7. Agreement of the Verb with its Subject. Principal exceptions to this general rule.

8. Use and place of Complements.

9. Use of Auxiliaries (principal rule).

10. Principal rule on the use of the Subjunctive.

11. Practical exercises on the use of the Tenses (without rules).

12. Essential difference between the Present Participle and the Verbal Adjective.

13. Recapitulation of the general rules and principal remarks on the agreement of the Past Participle.

14. N.B. As occasion offers, there will be taught, by means of Reading lessons, Dictations and Reproductions, the most important rules on Orthography, on the use of certain determinative Adjectives (vingt, cent, tout, quelque), of certain Pronouns (en, y, à, qui, auquel, d'on, dont, &c.), and of certain undeclined words (plutôt, plus tôt, parce que, par ce que, quoique, quoi que, quand quant).

Flemish.

1. Recapitulation by means of Reading lessons, and Dictation of the principal rules taught in the preceding stage.

2. Complex sentence. Principal and dependent clause. Co-ordinate and subordinate clauses. Principal rules of the use of the contracted sentence.

3. Special rules on Numerals and Pronouns. Inflection.

4. Difference between weak and strong conjugations in sentences containing strong and irregular Verbs.

5. Kinds of Verbs, classified according to their meaning.

6. Conversion of words, e.g. immer, nimmer; ooit, nooit; altijd, altoos; na, naar, &c. &c.

German.

1. Recapitulation by means of Reading lessons, and Dictation of the principal rules taught in the preceding stage.

2. Complex sentence. Principal and dependent clauses. Co-ordinate and subordinate clauses. Conjunctions. Contracted clauses. Punctuation.

3. Inflection of Numerals and Pronouns.

4. Difference between strong and weak conjugations in sentences containing strong and irregular Verbs.

5. Classification of Verbs according to their meaning. Verbs governing the Genitive, the Dative, the Accusative, the Dative and the Accusative.

Applications. Grammatical explanation of pieces read and previously studied for the sake of the sense.

Dictation (mostly in connected phrases) from classical authors. Exercise of invention.

IV. Derivations of words and Word-building taught during the Reading lessons; roots and radical words; compound words, derivative words; prefixes, suffixes, terminations. Kinship of words.

Homonyms, synonyms. Words used in different senses.

C.—Writing. . . . . .

Upper Primary Schools.

A.—Reading with expression.

Literary extracts selected for explaining the conception of the whole, its arrangement of ideas, and the expression. Reading with expression of pieces explained. Scientific reading.

Rendition of account, giving a summary of the reading recommended to the pupil by the teacher. Recitation with expression.

N.B. The teacher will give a short account of the author of the piece.

B.—Mother-tongue.

I. Elocution. The object of these exercises is to accustom the pupils to express easily, with clearness and precision, their own ideas derived from their own experience.

The subjects to be treated of are very various, and are mostly derived from explanations of their Reading lessons, from their reproductions, which are all the better for having previously been orally enlarged upon; also from their lessons on History, Natural Science, &c.

It must be remembered that the object is not to make the pupils recite from memory, but to lead them to express their own observations, ideas and emotions.

II. Composition.
- (a) Precepts. General quality of Style. Principal figures of speech. Rules of Composition applied to narrative, to description and to correspondence.
- (b) Study of Models. (See the Course of Reading.)
- (c) Exercises. Narratives, descriptions, comparisons, correspondence. Summary of lessons. Description of a walk or an excursion. Business letters.

III. Grammar. Complementary study of words by means of the Reading lessons or Dictation of passages from classical writers.

More complete study of the principal rules of Syntax.

Applications. Grammatical explanation of the Reading lessons. Oral grammatical analysis of Syntax. Exercises of invention.

IV. Study of Synonyms.

CANTON OF GENEVA.

First Stage.

Lessons on Intuition; telling stories; conversations and object lessons.

Reading. Simultaneous lessons on the black-board. Lessons from Pictures. These Picture-lessons are authorized only for schools of six stages. First Reading lessons in Primer.

Second Stage.

Continued reading from Primer. Pronunciation and enunciation (*"Articulation"*). Recitation (the master first reading the piece to the class and explaining words and sense).

Language. Transcription, dictation and explanation, and study of easy words. Dictation of Nouns followed by an Adjective or other qualification.

Short oral and written exercises of invention: the Noun being given, the children are required to find a suitable Adjective or other qualification, and vice versâ.

Third Stage.

Reading. Pronunciation, Liaison, Punctuation. Recitation (the master first reading the piece to the class and explaining words and sense). (Recitation of 50 verses each half.)

Language. Study of a vocabulary. Dictation. Exercises of invention; a Verb being given, to supply the subject, attribute, predicate and copula, and vice versâ.

Construction of simple phrases. Verbs: Present, Imperfect and simple Future of the Auxiliaries and of Verbs in *er* (parler). Noun with Adjective. Gender, Number. Formation of regular Plurals of the three kinds of words hitherto learnt. Agreement of Adjective and of Verb.

Fourth Stage.

Reading. Pronunciation and intonation. Study and recitation of very simple pieces (80 verses or lines of prose each half). (Two lessons a week.) Repeating from memory the sense of a piece read ("*compte rendu*"), (the master first reading the piece to the class and explaining the sense and the words).

Language. Study and explanation of words. Spelling by dictation. The sense of the words during dictation, and the application of the grammatical rules during correction, ought to furnish occasion for numerous exercises. Simple sentences formed by the pupils. Easy Compositions. Definite Article. Principal exceptions in the formation of plural of Nouns and Adjectives. Personal Pronouns. Conjugation of the first three Moods of Auxiliaries and the regular Verbs of the four Conjugations. Finding subject, verb, attribute and direct complement in the text of a piece dictated or read.

Fifth Stage.

Reading with expression, repeating subsequently from memory

the sense of the piece read (the master first reading it to the class, explaining the sense and the words). Study and recitation of 200 verses or lines.

Language. Study and explanation of words (see on this subject the instructions on Spelling by Dictation given in the Fourth Stage). Conjugation of Auxiliaries and regular Verbs. The commonest irregular Verbs. Elementary explanation of the use of Prepositions, Conjunctions and Adverbs. Finding subject, verb, attributes and complements, in the text of a piece dictated or read. Simple and co-ordinate sentences. Oral and written exercises on these two kinds of sentences. Composition. Imitation and frequent reproduction of short pieces recited.

Sixth Stage.

Reading. Reading with expression (see instructions given, from the Second Stage upwards). Reading extracts on the subject of Morals, History, Health, Natural History, Agriculture, Industries, &c., accompanied by explanations. Recitation of verse and prose (300 verses or lines), (two lessons of three quarters of an hour each per week).

Language. Study and explanation of words. Spelling by dictation (see instructions given on this subject in the Fourth Stage. Punctuation. Subordinate sentences. Conjugation of simple and compound Tenses. Irregular Verbs. Finding subject, verb, attribute and complements, in a piece dictated or read. Frequent exercises on various kinds of Composition. Oral and written exercises on the models selected from the Reading pieces.

HAMBURG.*

Standard I. Speaking exercises. Cultivating the power of observation. The division of words into syllables and syllables

* Taken from the "Report on Schools in Germany and Switzerland," by George B. Davis, Clerk to the Birmingham School Board.

into sounds. Reading written characters. Reading (to be practised both simultaneously and individually) with clear and correct pronunciation. Easy exercises in Orthography. Memory exercises. (These consist of easy recitations, and the practice of describing in simple language facts and circumstances within the child's knowledge.)

Standard II. Improved Reading, especially in regard to pronunciation and fluency. Practice in speaking correctly, by adding to the Reading lessons observations on the different points contained in them, as far as the child's knowledge will permit. Preliminary lessons as an introduction to the future study of Grammar. Orthographical exercises. Transcribing Reading lessons. Writing from dictation. Writing from memory passages contained in the Reading lessons. The composition of very easy sentences. Memory exercises.

Standard III. Clear and intelligent reading, and relating in the pupil's own words the subject matter of the Reading lessons. An outline knowledge of Declensions and Comparisons, and the conjugation of the chief tenses of the Verbs in both the Active and Passive voices. The construction of a simple proposition, and an introduction to the simpler form of enlarged sentences. Orthographical exercises. Easy Composition. Memory exercises.

Standard IV. Improved expression in Reading, with explanation of the passages read, and ability to reproduce in the scholar's own words the subject matter of the lesson. The Declensions, Comparisons and Conjugations. Enlarged Sentences, with some knowledge of word-building. The more important parts of speech. Exercises in style. Writing from memory the substance of a passage spoken or read. Orthographical exercises. Memory exercises.

Standard V. Reading with intelligence and expression. Practising the art of Speaking by relating again the subject matter of the Reading lessons. Further knowledge of enlarged sentences and an introduction to complex sentences. The Parts of Speech. Exercises in style as applied to descriptions and narrations. Composition of business and other letters of an easy character. Memory exercises.

Standard VI. Practising expressive Reading. The construction of Proposition. Word-building. Punctuation. Exercises in style. Composition of Narrations, Descriptions and Business letters. Memory exercises.

Standard VII. The Reading of difficult extracts from Classical literature. A general knowledge of the whole Grammar. Exercises in style. Composition as applied to business purposes and also easy Essays. Exercises in speaking, with special attention to the style of delivery and enunciation.

From Standard V. onwards the Poetry read consists of model pieces selected from the writings of the chief German authors; and a sufficient knowledge of the literary history has to be interwoven with the explanations to enable the children to understand the allusions contained in the several passages.

ITALY.

A.—*First Class* (Lower Section).

Italian Language. Graduated exercises in formation of syllables, analysing words selected for that purpose and explained. Formation of letters, syllables and words, by imitation. Writing from dictation words of simple syllables. Graduated lessons in reading and in correct pronunciation. Explanation of words and sentences read. Writing from copy or dictation.

Orthography. Memory exercises.

B.—*Second Class.*

Italian Language. Reading with ease and intelligence, with explanation of the matter read. Dictation and Orthography. Graduated exercises in Calligraphy.

Parts of Speech. Conjugation of auxiliary Verbs and of regular Verbs by means of sentences carefully selected to inculcate moral truths and to illustrate rules of grammar.* Elementary knowledge of Analysis. Short and easy composition by imitation exercises on the nomenclature of objects in daily use.

C.—*Third Class.*

Italian Language. Reading, with explanation of the matter read. Declension of Nouns and Adjectives. Conjugation of irregular and defective Verbs. Use of the Parts of Speech, and oral exercises in grammatical Analysis. Periods and Punctuation. Graduated exercises of Composition. Short tales, easy descriptions, letters. Exercises in nomenclature of objects in domestic use, of trades and arts.

Progressive exercises in Calligraphy. Memory exercises.

D.—*Fourth Class.*

Italian Language. Reading, with explanation of the matter read. Usual Grammar and exercises. Composition. Tales from the history of Italy, fables, descriptions, letters on various subjects. Nomenclature of objects in domestic use, of trades and arts.

Progressive exercises in Calligraphy. Memory exercises.

MUHLHAUSEN.

The Standards for Language are meagre, and as they refer principally to different sections of the authorized school-books, they offer little interest to the English reader.

* "Pray to God *and* keep your powder dry."—THE COMPILER.

NEUCHATEL.

1. Reading and Recitation.

(a) *Reading.* The Reading lessons are the most important of all the lessons given in the school, and the teacher is therefore bound to devote to them all the care they deserve. These lessons must only be given under the direction of a master, who before entering the school will attentively study the Reading lesson and prepare all that is to be said on it; it is always imprudent to trust to the inspiration of the moment.

Everything must be discussed in class—the subject-matter, the style, the moral idea underlying it; not a word or expression must be passed over without having its sense made clear to the child's mind; when opportunity offers, the teacher will add geographical and historical explanations; etymology, orthography and grammar will equally find frequent illustrations. Only by such means will the pupil acquire a good pronunciation, and learn to read with expression, because he will understand the general sense of the pieces read, and will identify himself with the ideas of the author. He will no longer read mere words, but ideas and things. Thus mere mechanical reading will as speedily as possible be followed by correct and intelligent reading.

The teacher will not fail to read to the class the piece to be studied, so that the pupils may acquire the desired intonation and expression. The subject-matter of everything read must be within the range of the child's capacity. . . .

Lower Grade.

First Year. Reading and Spelling.

Second Year. Fluent reading, with explanations. Pronunciation.

Intermediate Grade.

First Year. Fluent reading, with explanations. Pronunciation. Liaison. Oral reproduction of the matter read in the child's own words.

Second Year. The work of the preceding year, more advanced.

Upper Grade.

First Year. Fluent reading, with explanation. Pronunciation. Liaison. Intonation. Definitions. Oral reproduction of the matter read in the child's own words.

Second Year. The work of the preceding year, more advanced. Explanation of the leading principles of style.

Course of Recapitulation.

The same exercises and books as are used in the Upper Grades.

(*b*) *Recitations.* The pieces to be recited must first be read, explained and prepared by the master, so that the pupils should understand what they learn by heart, and be able to reproduce it in harmony with the context. From the outset the scholar should be made to give the right expression, as a bad habit once acquired is very difficult to be uprooted.

The recitations will be made *individually*, never *collectively*. Some of the pieces selected shall be connected prose, others dialogues. The scholars are sometimes to be called upon to recite in presence of the class, either from the teacher's desk or in front of the benches. Every pupil shall in turn be called out, even if it be for a very short piece. The same pieces will be learnt by the whole class; the selection shall not be left to the pupils. These recitations shall be practised the whole year round, and not merely at the approach of the examinations.

History, Grammar and Geography do not form parts of these recitations, and must therefore *not be learnt by heart*.

Lower Grade.

First and Second Years. Short pieces of prose and poetry.

Intermediate Grade.

First and Second Years. Prose and poetry.

Upper Grade.

First and Second Years. Prose, dialogues, different kinds of poetry.

2. Vocabulary.*

...... Generally there are given to the pupils about forty words a day to learn, say a whole column of words, without any explanation. If, on the contrary, the teacher beforehand explains the meaning of every word, and requires that the scholar should after private study be able at the next lesson to repeat from memory the spelling and the definition of the words thus prepared, then the study of the Vocabulary will prove truly fruitful. This procedure is very earnestly recommended to the Teaching body.

To extend the children's vocabulary, the teacher will utilize the object lessons; he will draw their attention to the kinship of words; he will lead them to form little sentences with the words learnt; from time to time dictation will take the place of oral spelling. . . . .

Lower Grade.
First and Second Years. Ten to fifteen words at a time.

Intermediate Grade.
First and Second Years. Fifteen to twenty words at a time.

Upper Grade.
First and Second Years. Twenty to thirty words at a time.

3. Grammar, Orthography and Analysis.

(*a*) *Grammar.* The Grammar lessons must be each time prepared in class by the master. In testing this work, he will question the pupils, so as to prevent mere learning by rote.

(*b*) In all the Grades, the exercises in *Orthography* will as a rule be a practical application of the Grammar lessons; the dictations are not to be chosen at haphazard from the first book at hand, as they would have no bearing on one another, nor on the chapter of Grammar just studied. The dictations are to be short and graduated; the corrections are to be made in class by

---

* The omitted matter, indicated by dots, refers solely to local matters, such as the manuals recommended and the sections for each year's study.

the pupil himself, strictly watched and guided by the teacher. This will teach the pupils to attend to accents and punctuation. The master will always exact that the dictations be written neatly. This remark applies to all written exercises, dictations, compositions, calculations, copies, conjugations, &c. . . . .

(c) *Analysis.* Analysis is to be a recapitulation of the lessons already learnt in Grammar and applied in Dictation. What people have agreed to call *grammatical* and *logical* Analysis will be taught simultaneously, the distinction having no raison d'être; for this reason the dictations must have a bearing on the Grammar lessons. In any case, all Analysis must be oral.

There are two kinds of Analysis; the first consists in taking up the words one by one to tell the parts of speech, giving their several functions in the phrase later on. This is the *analytic* method followed by Larousse. It is long and wearying; if children as a rule dislike Analysis, it is due to this manner of teaching.

The *synthetic* method, on the contrary, proceeds very differently. The pupil's attention is first of all drawn to the simple sentence and to the essential parts composing it, be it the Verb or the Noun. Example: "The shepherd sings." Then the sentence is expanded by the addition of the completion of the Predicate: "The shepherd sings a melody." Next come the indirect Object and the extensions of the Predicate: "The shepherd sings a melody in the forest;" and next follows the Adjective: "The good shepherd sings a beautiful melody in the depth of the forest." Next comes the Personal Pronoun: "The good shepherd, &c.; he watches the little lambs, &c."

When once, by means of numerous exercises, the child can, so to speak, count up the ideas expressed in a sentence, when he can distinguish between *being, quality, action,* or noun, adjective and verb, we can teach the Singular and Plural of Nouns, but only in the completion of the sentence, leaving the subject in the Singular: "The shepherd sings melodies in the forests on the hill-slopes." Lastly comes the agreement of the Adjective: "The shepherd sings beautiful melodies in the dense forests on the steep hill-slopes."* . . . .

As yet we have no manuals of dictation on the basis of the synthetic method, but with effort and goodwill this defect is easily supplied.

The employment of the synthetic method is earnestly recommended, because progress will be more rapid. To facilitate its introduction, the Education Committees† must not fail to do their part; they must bear in mind the attempts made by the teacher, and in their examinations not give any dictations but such as fit into the general framework of the lessons given to the class. It is evident that if an examination in Dictation, given to a class of juniors, bristles with participles and with applications of rules that have not yet occurred in the course gone through, there will be numerous faults and hardly any analysis, the child finding himself in presence of difficulties which he has not studied.

Lower Grade.

First Year. Grammar. Oral lessons in connection with the exercises in Orthography.

Orthography. Copying in a separate copy-book words to be learnt by heart. Transcription from the Reading-book. Dictation of short detached sentences, first with a Noun for subject, then with Adjectives, &c., on the sequence indicated above (" The shepherd sings," &c.).

Analysis. Exercises on Analysis to test grammatical knowledge.

Second Year. Grammar. Oral lessons bearing on the exercises on Orthography.

---

* Here follows a long paragraph still more peculiar to the French language; but enough has been shown to indicate the minute instructions given by the Education Ministry of Neuchâtel to both teachers and Inspectors. It is all the difference between a guidance-affording Ministry and a mere administrative Department.

† Note the expression, "Education Committees." Inspectors inspect but do not examine.

Orthography. The same exercises as last year, in addition to making a clean copy of the corrected exercises. Transcription from memory of a piece of prose or poetry. Conjugation by sentences of the verbs *être* and *avoir* in the simple tenses of the indicative and imperative.

Analysis. Exercises on Nouns and Pronouns used as Subjects; also on the Adjective and on the Verb.

Intermediate Grade.

First Year. Grammar. Chapter having bearing on the exercises on Orthography.

Orthography. Transcription of words, with short explanations. Dictations on Nouns, Adjectives, Personal Pronouns and Verbs (simple tenses of Indicative and Imperative). Home exercises on Grammar. Copies of dictations carefully made. Conjugation by means of sentences of simple Tenses, and of regular Verbs of the First Conjugation.

Analysis. Decomposition of a complex sentence into simple sentences. Subject, Verb, completion of the object. Parsing of Article, Noun, Adjective, Pronoun and Verb.

Second Year. Grammar. The same exercises as in the year preceding.

Orthography. Copying words, with short explanations. The same dictations. Simple and compound Tenses of the Indicative and Imperative of the verbs *être* and *avoir*, and of the regular Verbs of the First Conjugation. Home exercises in Grammar. Clean copy of dictations. Words in common use of like sound and different meaning of common occurrence.

Analysis. The same as last year.

Upper Grade.

First Year. Grammar. Chapters bearing on the exercises on Orthography.

Orthography. Transcription of words that have been explained. Dictation on the chief difficulties in the rules of agreement.

Nouns, Adjectives, Pronouns, regular Verbs, and the commonest irregular Verbs and Participles. Home lessons in Grammar. Clean copies of dictation. Words of like sound and different meaning. Families of words (provide, providence, provident, prudent, prude, prudential, province, provincial, &c. &c.). Derivations. Irregularities of derivation.

Analysis. Decomposition of a compound sentence into simple sentences; subject, predicate, completion of object, direct and indirect. Parsing all the parts of speech.

Second Year. Grammar. The same exercises as last year.

Orthography. The same exercises as last year. Dictation on the ten parts of speech.

Analysis and Parsing. Classification of Prepositions. Parsing all parts of speech.

4. ELOCUTION AND COMPOSITION.

(*a*) *Elocution Exercises* are rarely practised in our classes; thus the child remains entirely passive; he is not called upon to act for himself, to speak, to overcome that timidity which is injurious to so many people. Therefore teachers are earnestly advised to give speaking lessons. At all times and in all the lessons, they should insist on answers consisting of complete sentences, taking care to correct errors of expression, bad pronunciation and local faults. As in recitations, so here the child will be called upon to speak in presence of his class-mates, either from the teacher's desk or in front of the benches, care being taken to maintain discipline.

Lower Grade.

First and Second Years. Short recitation by the pupil, either of a piece read, or of a fact narrated by the master, and a variety of similar exercises.

Intermediate Grade.

First Year. The same exercises as in the Lower Grade. A sentence being given as theme, the pupil is called upon to express the same idea in a variety of ways, or by means of equivalents and synonyms.

Second Year. The same exercises as last year. Change an assertion into a question or an exclamation, or express it dubitatively, and vice versâ.

Upper Grade.

First and Second Years. The same exercises as last year. Development of a theme—proposed sometimes by the pupils, and sometimes by the teacher.

(*b*) *Composition.* The exercises in composition and style will be previously discussed in class between teacher and pupils; he will lead them to find out the ideas to be developed; if need be, he will point them out, as well as the sequence in which they ought to be treated; in a word, he will prepare the framework of the subject-matter of the exercise.

The teacher will not lose sight of these three steps to be always taken: 1st, establish the ideas; 2nd, arrange them in proper sequence; 3rd, find suitable expression for them.

The compositions and the corrections must be done in class. From time to time, and when the examinations approach, the pupils will have themes given them to work out independently, without any previous help from the master. It is recommended that clean copies be made of the compositions, and these must be regularly corrected. The teacher will also draw the pupils' attention to the form to be given to a letter, and to the care required by this kind of composition.

Lower Grade.

First Year. Object lesson. Conversation. Training of the powers of observation by means of lessons on objects surrounding the child. Oral exercise on the names of things, their uses, mechanisms, &c.; or if animals, names, movements, qualities, actions, uses, &c. Exercises on simple affirmative, negative and interrogative sentences. Exercises on objects taken from family life, the house, the town, the village, the country. The master will teach or make the pupils find out the names of the objects in school, in the workshop, &c.; the names of domestic and wild animals; of aquatic, carnivorous and herbivorous animals; of animals active by day and those active at night, &c.; of fresh and salt water fish; of garden plants, edible vegetables, flowers, fruits, poisonous plants, orchards and forests; geographical names; streams, rivers, lakes, seas, mountains, towns, &c. Incite the children to discuss the form and use of objects, their colour, the habits of animals, &c. Example: What is the shape of the garden? It is square, fertile, productive, large, full of flowers, beautiful, neglected, arid, &c. Or, What kind of work does the horse do? It runs, draws loads, carries, jumps, ploughs, neighs, runs forward, backs, &c.

Second Year. The same exercises, oral and in writing. Write five or six sentences on a given Noun (animal, plant, fish, bird, &c.); these sentences to be varied both in words and in form, and to consist of only subject and verb, and afterwards of subject, verb and complement.

Intermediate Grade.

First Year. Recapitulation of exercises of preceding year. Sentences on a given Noun to consist of subject, verb, direct and indirect object and enlargement of object. Writing from memory a tale or fable previously told or read by the teacher.

Second Year. Short essays on easy subjects known to the pupil and previously explained by the teacher.

Upper Grade.

First Year. Continuation of the exercises of preceding years.

Second Year. Various kinds of composition; tales; descriptions; geographical and historical subjects; business and family letters; agreements, &c.

Recapitulatory Course.

The same exercises as in previous years, devoting special attention to letter-writing.

PRUSSIA.

FIRST STANDARD (11 hours out of 22).

The teaching begins with intuitive lessons (*Anschauungsübungen*), the material for which is supplied by the school, the house, the dwelling-place, the field, the meadow, the wood. The children first learn the names of the things shown them, either in nature or in pictures, and are then trained to observe them closely, and to express their observations in complete sentences.

The teacher must insist on distinct and pure speech, correct formation of the phrase, and due intonation in accordance with the sense.

The practices in *vivâ voce* expression are not to constitute a separate course; they are preparatory to the instruction in reading and writing, and accompany it on its further stages.

Instruction in Writing and Reading is to be given in accordance with the method introduced in the Training Schools of the district; Reading by spelling is forbidden.

After the first six months the children must be able to analyse easy phrases into words, the words into syllables, and the syllables into sounds; they must be able to write the letters representing these respective sounds, and to read what they have written.

In the latter part of the first half-year the children begin to learn the printed letters. In the second half-year they learn all the printed letters, the names of the letters with their long and short sounds.

As soon as the children are able to read single words, they must be trained to attach a distinct idea to each word, and when they read sentences a distinct sense to each phrase, so as to prevent the formation of the habit of mere mechanical, unthinking reading.

In teaching Writing the teacher shows on the black-board the genesis of the letter, and discusses the component parts, so as to facilitate the copying of it.

At first it is sufficient if the children write legibly and pretty regularly. In a special course the single letters and their combinations into words are in suitable gradations again discussed and practised.

After the first year children must be able to read, with correct enunciation, easy sentences in written and printed characters, to transcribe them without mistake, to analyse short sentences, written on the black-board, into words, the words into syllables, and to write them with tolerable accuracy. The First Part of the Primer *(Fibel)* must be finished.

SECOND STANDARD (11 hours out of 22).

In the Second Standard children are required to read not only with tolerable fluency and correct pronunciation, but also in harmony with the sense of the piece, paying attention to the punctuation; they are expected to answer questions on the contents, and to some extent connectedly to reproduce small narratives; they are also to transcribe from the Reading-book free of error; they are to have some practice in Dictation, and be able to write down correctly from memory small sentences read or told them, as well as proverbs and aphorisms learnt by heart.

The children must be able pretty neatly to write small letters and capitals. Spelling is to be perfected, and for this purpose special lessons are given in connection with the Reading-book and with the intuition lessons *(Anschauungsunterricht)*.

Subjects for Intuition lessons are selected chiefly from the Reading-book; objects and occurrences treated of in the Reading lessons are discussed and rendered visible as much as possible.

THIRD STANDARD (8 hours out of 28).

Practice in fluent reading with correct pronunciation is kept up; greater attention is devoted to the contents; right intonation and appreciation of what has been read is more and more striven after.

The pupils are trained to and practised in orally and connectedly reproducing the matter read; in this they will naturally make use of the phraseology of the book; but they are to be encouraged by questions to paraphrase expressions, to alter the form of whole phrases, so as to put the subject-matter into a form consonant with their own conceptions and their own standpoint.

A few prose pieces and several poems to be learnt by heart.

A special series of lessons to be given in Orthography.

Additional attention is devoted to Writing. Children begin partly to use the pen.

In *Grammar* the children will learn the formation of the Plural of Nouns, forming sentences where the Subjects are spoken of in singular and in plural; what they are, how they are, and what they do. The children will also learn Verbs and Adjectives, applying them in sentences. In Word-building they will learn the easier derivations by means of suffixes: chen = kin (as lambkin); lein = ling (as worldling); ig = y (as thirsty); lich = ly (as lordly); isch = ish (as heathenish).

FOURTH STANDARD (8 hours out of 28).

More advanced requirements in fluent reading, correct pronunciation, and clear understanding of the difficult pieces in the Reading-book for intermediate classes.

In *Grammar*. Study of Compound and Derivative words, taught mostly by the teacher's use of them, in connected speech, where their significance is instantly recognized. At times the sense must be given in paraphrases.

Also all the cases of the Noun with Definite and Indefinite Article, and the degrees of Comparison of the Adjective, with applications in sentences.

In *Composition*. Simple descriptions of objects and of events;

short parables or fables, and reproductions in writing of a story told to the children. Writing down from memory narratives and descriptions read, but not learnt by heart. Every exercise is to be previously discussed between teacher and pupils; the latter being led verbally to express their ideas and perceptions in suitable form, and gradually more and more connected.

These written exercises are at the earlier stages to be rendered easier by leading questions and hints being written upon the black-board; but this practice is to be gradually abandoned.

Children in the Fourth Standard are to be able to write a short composition without any prompting, after the teacher has supplied the subject-matter, discussed it in its sequence of ideas, has practised the grammatical form, and has made the necessary observations on spelling and punctuation.

FIFTH STANDARD (8 hours out of 30).

(a) *Reading* (3 hours). Practice in Reading continued, in the Reading-book for the Senior Classes. Severer demands on intelligence, intonation, and apprehension of the subject-matter. Accurate learning by heart of several pieces of poetry.

(b) *Spelling* (1 hour). Greater accuracy in Orthography. Ability to write from memory without any serious error a reading lesson learnt by heart.

(c) *Writing* (1 hour). Special study of the forms of capitals and small letters. Writing from copy set.

The Senior Classes also practise the Roman characters.

(d) *Grammar* (1 hour). Tenses of Verb and Imperative Mood; both applied in sentences. Transposition of a sentence from the Active into the Passive Voice and conversely.

The most important parts of the Study of Words; the simple sentence and its component parts.

(e) *Composition* (2 hours). Practice as in Fourth Standard, but with more advanced requirements.

SIXTH STANDARD (8 hours out of 32).

(a) *Reading* (3 hours). The two sections of this course read together. This course of two years must carry the student through at least sixty extracts (*Lesestücke*) in such a manner that they not only can read them well, but also understand them in their leading ideas and in the connection of the several parts. Great attention is to be devoted to verbal rendering of the main thoughts in connected and fluent speech.

A free form of reproduction is to be gradually acquired.

Poetry to be learnt by heart; especially selected from the classical works of German poets, and also from popular poets.

Some account of the national poets since the time of the Reformation.

Final Aim. In this highest Standard the pupils are to be able to read at sight, fluently and with expression, somewhat difficult pieces, whose contents, however, are not too remote from their sphere of life.

They must also be able correctly to reproduce longer pieces of composition.

(b) *Spelling* (1 hour). Readiness in Orthography, Signs and Punctuation, to be imparted in Reading, Grammar and Composition.

If certain errors recur frequently, it is to be regarded as a sign that the corresponding lessons are to be gone over again.

Special attention is to be devoted to words of like sound and different meaning, to the spelling and meaning of foreign words in common use. All such exercises to be applied in sentences.

Punctuation to advance *pari passu* with analysis of sentences.

(c) *Grammar* (2 hours). Repetition and expansion of the work of the Fifth Standard.

Also different forms of speech, or modes of expression. Participles, use of Adjectives with Definite, Indefinite, and without any Article; the use of the Numerals, of the Possessive, Demonstrative and Interrogative Pronouns.

PRUSSIA. 97

The simple sentence with enlargement of Subject, extension of Predicate, enlargement of Object; and the different kinds of subordinate sentences.

Examples are mostly to be taken out of the Reading-book.

(*d*) *Composition.* Free reproduction of extracts read; précis; descriptions and comparisons of subjects taken from all branches of study.

Reproduction of lessons on Naturkunde, Geography and German History.

The written solution of some problems in Arithmetic also is very suitable as a practice in clear exposition. The more advanced pupils may be encouraged to write short essays, in illustration of proverbs, and the like.

Simple letters and the usual business forms, such as schedules, receipts, accounts, advertisements, certificates, testimonials, and the like. The pupils are to be taught the proper place for the date, &c., of letters, and above all the address on the cover for posting, &c. Occasionally letters are to be handed in to the teacher ready for post (*postfertig*).

Extract from the Circular of the Government of Arnsberg, dated August 2nd, 1879.

Once a week the pupils will hand in for correction alternately an essay and an exercise on Orthography. These themes are to be numbered by the pupils, the date being written in the margin. Correction is to be made out of school hours, the errors being underlined in coloured ink, and afterwards corrected by the pupils themselves. The teacher will give an award to every such exercise. Neat transcription of fully corrected exercises is not to be made.*

* This regulation cannot be too highly commended, honest exercise-books affording to the Inspector, as well as to the parents, the best record and index of the amount and quality of the work done in the school. See also note on p. 100.—The Compiler.

SAXONY.

Instruction in language aims at training children both to understand High German, and to use it correctly in speech as well as writing.* But it aims also at elevating the hearts and minds of our youth by introducing them to our popular literature. For this reason, training in language is to be kept in view in all lessons, besides those specially set apart for this object.†

Instruction in Language comprises : Exercise in Speaking, Reading, Writing, and—as a means to an end—an elementary knowledge of German Grammar. These branches are to be placed in correlation to each other.

(*a*) *Exercise in Speaking.* These exercises aim at training the pupils, on the one hand, to speak with purity and distinctness, and, on the other hand, to acquire ease, accuracy and precision in the expression of their ideas. This is done in the early stages principally by means of lessons on Intuition, and later on mainly by means of the subject-matter of the Reading lesson.

Select portions of prose and poetry, to be learnt by heart and repeated with expression by the pupils of every Stage.‡

Foot-notes of the German original.

* According to law, and obviously, "within the range of the children's ideas, observation and general knowledge."

† The law adds that "the teacher must by reading awaken in the pupils the desire to continue their self-culture."

‡ In the Elementary Classes, the lessons on Intuition offer the best opportunity for teaching a few little verses, whose text has reference to the subject-matter of the lessons. Great care will have to be taken in selecting these pieces to exclude triviality; it is easy to mistake childish for childlike things, the boundary-line being very faint. Our juvenile literature offers a large choice of excellent pieces. To what extent Froebel's method is to be introduced is impossible to determine on general principles. That here and there good results have been attained by it is certain; the children delight in the unusual stimulus to which even dull natures cannot be wholly insensible. Mere experiments, however, are to be decidedly discountenanced.

In the more advanced stages, the pieces to be learnt by heart and recited

The acquisition of ease in expression is to be striven after by insisting on complete answers to questions in the lessons on *all* subjects; by repetition of stories and descriptions; by concise solutions of problems, and by giving a synopsis of a chain of reasoning.

In Wendic schools, it must be insisted on from the earliest school years that the children should learn to speak German also.*

(*b*) *Reading.* The object of the Reading lessons is to enable the children to read suitable matter in German and Roman† characters fluently, distinctly, with proper pronunciation and enunciation, paying attention to the stops, and understanding the subject-matter read at least in every essential point.

Besides the Reading-machine and the Primer,‡ the school ought to use a Reading-book containing pieces popular in tone, and unexceptionable both for matter and style.

At the end of the second year, the children must have attained perfect ease in reading of words and sentences; in the subsequent years the selections are steadily to increase in difficulty.

Even in the earliest elementary stages, the children must be trained to pay intelligent heed to punctuation and to accent and stress. To promote the habit of reading with intelligence, the teacher will not fail at every stage carefully to discuss with the

are naturally selected from and follow upon the discussion of the Reading lessons; these pieces are then to be committed to memory by the whole class.

The pieces to be learnt by heart should to a great extent be selected for their national popular colouring. A store of good popular poetry, acquired and affectionately remembered by the school-children all over the country, would certainly not fail to exert an ennobling influence on the life of the people.

* On this point the law enjoins on the teachers great caution and circumspection; it points out that the problem is difficult, but can be solved to universal satisfaction if the teachers proceed with skill and gentle forbearance.

† The Roman characters are not to be taught till the second year.

‡ The law demands that the Primer used in the school shall be on the most approved modern methods, but does not state which Primer or which method is to be preferred. Thus, for the first year, the teacher has full latitude given him in the choice of his book.

class the subject-matter read in the lesson. In the senior classes the teacher may in these conversations give some account of German poets.

(c) *Writing.* The instruction in Writing consists of three branches, viz. Calligraphy, Spelling and Composition. These exercises are to support each other mutually; neatness of execution to be persistently enforced. The compositions to be carefully corrected,* and the corrections to be discussed in class.

1. The exercises in Calligraphy aim at the acquisition of a simple, legible, flowing and pleasant handwriting. In the first school year, Writing is taught in connection with Reading; in the second and subsequent school years, the instruction in Writing is given in special lessons..... Instruction in Writing is to be given mostly on the method known as Taktschrift (see p. 16 of "School Boards and Board Schools," by A. Sonnenschein).

2. .... Spelling is to be taught by transcription; by writing from memory, and according to definite rules of Orthography; and by dictation.

3. Lessons on Composition aim at imparting to pupils the skill to write down their thoughts correctly and orderly. They begin formally in the third year, foundation having been laid in the earlier years by the exercises in Speaking. Fit subjects for practice are, simple stories, descriptions, analogies, letters and business documents. The Reading lessons will most frequently offer subjects for composition, but at times also other lessons, as well as

* With reference to corrections, the law demands of the teacher punctuality, accuracy, neatness, appropriate comments in the margin, an award at the end according to well-known principles, and re-examination of the corrections made by the pupil.

In correcting, the following principles must be observed : (*a*) The teacher must distinguish between errors which the pupil at his stage of knowledge might have avoided, and such as are evidently accounted for by insufficiency of knowledge. (*b*) Errors of the first kind the teacher will simply underline, calling upon the pupil to correct them himself; errors of the second kind the teacher will correct himself and discuss with the scholar. (*c*) Corrections to be made either in the margin or at the end.

current events and the pupil's own experiences. The themes are first to be carefully discussed, both as to subject-matter and style, gradually, however, more and more emancipating the pupils at the successive stages.*

(*d*) *German Grammar.* The instruction in German Grammar imparts and practically applies as much knowledge of Grammar as is absolutely indispensable for a right comprehension and use of the German language.†

Grammar, properly so called, does not begin till the third school year; but a foundation has been laid in the previous years by the lessons in Speaking (Sprechübungen).‡

In the third and fourth years it is sufficient to combine on consecutive plan the grammatical instruction with the practices in Speaking, Reading and Writing. Special Grammar lessons are to be given in the later years.

The course begins with the study of the simple sentence, and afterwards—in the fourth year—it passes on to the study of the enlarged, compound and contracted sentence.§

* The law requires that the preparation of themes for composition be made with extreme care, so that the pupils may gain a clear insight into the logical sequence of ideas, the various modes of expression, and the requisite rules of Grammar and Spelling. To make sure of his point, the teacher is advised in each case to let oral exercise precede the writing of the theme, making his first corrections on the piece as it is spoken.

† "Those portions of Grammar which are not of importance for the right understanding and correct use of the language, are to be excluded from the curriculum of the Elementary School" (einfache Volksschule).

‡ In these lessons on Speaking, Reading and Writing, the teacher's principal aim will be to develope and cultivate a proper instinct for the language (Sprachgefühl), which afterwards finds its justification in the theories taught in the third and subsequent years.

§ "In the lowest stage the children learn the Noun, Article and Adjective; in the intermediate stage the difference between Singular and Plural, the cases of Nouns, the comparison of Adjectives, the principal tenses, persons, moods and voices of Verbs, and the simple sentence and its members. In the higher stage the pupils study the remaining parts of speech (Pronouns, Numerals, Adverbs, Prepositions and Conjunctions), Declensions and Conjugations, the

It follows that the different courses of study (rules on sentence, words and word-building) are best pursued on the plan of concentric gradual expansion, and must be persistently applied and illustrated in the lessons on Speaking, Reading and Writing.

CANTON DE VAUD.

Lower Grade (about 2 years).

A.—Exercises on Intuition and Language.

Intuitive teaching bears principally on the objects to be found in the school and at home; on the human body; on animals and plants with which the child is most familiar; also on the subdivisions of time; on trades and professions; families and degrees of kinship; epochs of life, &c.

The teacher will give short accounts of these subjects, and the children will orally reproduce them.

B.—Exercises combined with Writing and Reading.

Study of the first Reading-sheets, printed either in written or in Roman characters. The pupils will read on the black-board words of one or two syllables, and will reproduce them in writing. These exercises are afterwards continued with words of several syllables and with short sentences.

different kinds of sentences, and as much of word-building as is intelligible to children and practically useful. . . . . Centre of all Grammar lessons is the study of the sentence. In the lower classes it is sufficient to teach the simple sentence and the simplest forms of its enlargement by the required parts of speech; also the most essential parts of the formation of sounds and syllables (Laut- und Silbenlehre), and the formation of compound Nouns. In the upper classes, the enlarged simple sentence, the correlation of sentences, the contracted sentence, together with the necessary parts of speech; also declension of Nouns and Pronouns, and the most important rules on the derivation and composition of words (families of words)." All these lessons are based on intuition (Anschauung) and on the child's own experience. (See Wangemann's works on Language.)

Learning by heart pieces of poetry and of easy prose taken from the Reading-book. Study of an abridged collection of words. Numerous exercises on Orthography. Themes and transcriptions.

C.—Grammatical Exercises.

Elementary study of the Substantive, Verb, Article, Adjective and Personal Pronoun. Essential rules on Gender and Number. Formation of the plural of Nouns, and the plural and feminine of Adjectives. Conjugation of the simple tenses of the Indicative of the verbs *être* and *avoir*, and of the verbs of the First Conjugation. These Conjugations to be practised, sometimes orally, sometimes in writing, adding to the verb an attribute, or a direct, indirect or circumstantial complement.

Intermediate Grade (2 to 3 years).

A.—Continuation of the Exercises on Intuition and Language.

The teacher will exact more frequently than in the Lower Grade that the pupils should reproduce, either orally or in writing, the subject-matter of the lesson, and he will pay particular attention to the correction of the language and style.

B.—Reading, Recitation, Exercises in Orthography and Composition.

Fluent reading. Numerous exercises to ensure reading with intelligence and expression.

Learning by heart a selection of poems and of pieces of prose. Study of a collection of words larger than in the Lower Grade.

Numerous exercises in Orthography. Elementary exercises in Composition, combined with those on Intuition and Language.

C.—Grammar.

Syntax. Simple proposition. Enlarged proposition, i.e. with one or several complements.

Etymology. Different kinds of Nouns. Different classes of Articles, or determinative Adjectives. Qualifying Adjectives. Pronouns and their classification. Verbs. Conjugation of a large number of Verbs in sentences, first of simple, then of compound, tenses of the Indicative; all four Conjugations. Prepositions. Adverbs. The most important Synonyms.

Exercises on invention bearing on the study of the simple sentence and of various kinds of words.

Upper Grade (3 to 4 years).

A.—Reading, Recitation, Exercises in Orthography and Composition.

Fluent reading, with analysis of the subject-matter read. Numerous themes to familiarize the pupils with the essential rules of grammar.

B.—Grammar.

Syntax. Continuation of the study of sentences. Compound sentences. Co-ordinate and subordinate clauses.

Etymology. Study of Conjunctions, conjunctive Adverb and relative Pronoun. Moods used in compound sentences: Subjunctive, Conditional, Infinitive, Participles. Conjugation of all the tenses and moods of regular and irregular Verbs.

Exercises of invention bearing on the compound sentence and on Etymology.

Modification of sentences, i.e. exercises on the changes they can be made to undergo with respect to number, gender, person, tense, &c.

Recapitulation, analytic and methodic, of Etymology and Syntax.

For the most advanced Pupils.

Study of the principal difficulties and anomalies presented by the number and gender of Nouns. Collective Nouns, compound Nouns. Irregular formations of the feminine Adjective. Use of the pronouns le, la, en, y, tout, chacun, &c. Present Participle and verbal Adjective. Agreement of the Past Participle (Past Participle of reflective Verbs; followed by an infinitive, with the pronouns le, en; between que . . . . que, &c). Principal rules on the use of the tenses of the Indicative and Subjunctive. Difficulties in the use of certain invariable words (adverbs, prepositions, conjunctions). Punctuation. Principal Synonyms. Errors of speech of most common prevalence.

Observations.

The course of instruction in the mother-tongue prescribed in these Standards differs considerably from that which is generally followed in schools. While most grammars, servilely following the analytic method, successively pass under review the ten parts of speech, we study them in the order they present themselves in the sentence, and accordingly we begin with the syntax and the study of words.

The antiquated system is no doubt very convenient for the teacher, who is well acquainted with it and runs no risk of forgetting a single point, but it has the grave defect of being too abstract and too arid for beginners. Starting as it does from the general to descend to the particular, it does violence to the child's mind, which requires the contrary process, viz. to start from the particular and rise to the general and abstract, that is to say, to rule and theory. Children do not merely require to be acquainted with grammatical formulœ, but with the language itself, for the study of which grammar is but a means and an instrument. "Education," Pestalozzi says, "must lead the child by his own efforts to build up the science from its elements, that is to say, he must create it, in some sort invent it." It is this natural and progressive method which we have endeavoured to follow in our programme of studies. Accordingly we begin with the simplest combinations. . . . .*

* The omitted passages indicated by dots have reference to French Grammar, and are not likely to interest English readers.

ZURICH.

First Standard.

A.—PRELIMINARY PRACTICE IN THINKING AND SPEAKING.

1. Intuition and accurate apprehension, with name and description, of objects in the school-room, or of other objects well known to the children, and which can be exhibited in the school either in nature or in good pictures. The children are to name their most important properties, their uses, preparation, and what changes they may undergo, &c.: all in very simple little sentences, to be expressed with clear utterance, and to be impressed on the children by varied questions and by frequent repetition, both by individuals and by the class.

2. In immediate connection with the above, search of a larger number of objects known to the children, which stand in some relationship to those already discussed; all in short little sentences, with special attention to the right use of Singular and Plural.

N.B. These Exercises in Thinking and Speaking are to be gone through independently, not in connection with the Reading and Writing lessons. At the end of the course, the words or names of things so learnt can be made use of in teaching Reading and Writing.

B.—READING AND WRITING.

1. *Special Exercise preliminary to Reading.* Training of the ear and of the organs of speech in the correct appreciation and pure enunciation of the vowels both separately and in words; also the consonants both as initial and terminal sounds, and thereupon frequent practice in analysis of syllables consisting of 2, 3, or 4 sounds, and of polysyllabic words into syllables. Recomposition of sounds into syllables and words.

2. *Special Exercise preliminary to Writing.* Vertical, horizontal, and oblique lines; straight and curved lines to connect

given points, and free imitations of lines in various directions, single and in combinations; at first slowly, then quickly, and upon word of command.* Special attention to be given to correct posture of body and position of hand.

3. *Writing - Reading Instruction (Schreibleseunterricht).* † Sounds and signs of vowels, in sequence of progressive difficulty, with immediate application to combinations so soon as a given sign is understood; both initially and terminally, first in syllables of two sounds, then of more than two sounds; all this, together with the sounds of letters made either by the children or by the teacher, being the first practice in reading Written hand.

In the second half of this year, practice of Capital letters; and towards the end of the year, utilization, for Reading and Writing, of the words occurring in the exercises on Thinking and Speaking.

Second Standard.

A.—Practice in Thinking and Speaking.

1. Intuition, name and description of School and Home; ditto of other objects from the child's surroundings, which can be easily shown and examined, but especially of such objects as have life and growth, to be met with usually out of the house, viz., in the garden, in the field and in the wood; i.e. plants and animals, distinguishing their parts and their peculiarities of form, dwelling specially on their several properties and characteristics; in simple grammatical sentences, first .in presence of the object or its picture, and subsequently appealing solely to the imagination of the pupils.

2. In immediate connection with the above, search of other

---

* i. e. Taktschrift (see p. 100).

† i. e. Reading taught by Writing. The controversy between the advocates of the Schreibleseunterricht and of the Leseschreibunterricht is now practically decided in favour of the former; in England we are not ripe yet even to commence the discussion.

objects related to those already examined, utilizing the knowledge already acquired.

B.—READING AND WRITING.

1. *Reading and Writing* of the names of the objects examined, their properties and uses; and of short phrases describing these objects, properties and uses, from written and printed copies set.

2. In Reading: transition to a knowledge of Print and first practice in the same, within the sphere of the knowledge acquired in the above exercises. Gradual reading of words and phrases which have not yet been discussed, and, in the latter part of the year, reading of short descriptions and simple narratives, as an exercise partly in reading and partly in intelligent appreciation of the matter read, and with the view of increasing the store of words to be written.

3. Similar gradual transition to Writing of words and phrases, not set as copies, but which have occurred previously and are now only repeated to them.

Third Standard.

A.—PRACTICE IN THINKING AND SPEAKING.

1. Intuition, name and description of the immediate visible surroundings of the child, the whole village and its several parts, the surrounding meadows, fields, woods, &c. &c.

B.—READING AND WRITING.

Reading of simple descriptions of subjects similar or identical with those that have occurred under A, and of short narratives and small poems connected with them; oral repetition of the matter read, partly in the child's own words and partly in reply to questions.

Writing of descriptions and narratives, partly after copy set, partly from dictation by the teacher, and partly from memory, &c.

Fourth Standard.

Realschule* (Intermediate Classes).

1. *Reading and Explanation.* Reading of the scientific subjects fixed for this Standard from the domains of Geography, History, Naturkunde, as well as of a careful selection of pieces of poetry, which may have some bearing on the scientific subjects read, or may simply alternate with them. Explanation of notions which are still new to the pupils, also of more difficult phrases and peculiar expressions pointing out the sequence of ideas in the piece read.

2. *Grammar.* The simple Sentence; distinguishing Subject and Predicate in all kinds of phrases; those parts of speech which mostly serve as subjects and predicates; Number and Gender of Nouns; Person and Number of Verb; Number, Gender and degree of comparison of Adjectives; and, finally, simple expansion of the Verb and Adjective, and knowledge of the influence of the Noun consequent on this. All in sharply defined rules, based on a selection of model sentences made for the purpose, with perpetual application of what is already known, both orally and in writing; finding parallel passages in the reading lessons already gone through, &c.

3. *Composition.* In addition to the practices above enumerated, short descriptions and narratives, partly dictated by the teacher, but principally independent paraphrase of a piece of reading, and original composition on a subject previously discussed with or narrated by the teacher.

Fifth Standard.

1. *Reading and Explanation.* Reading of the scientific subjects appointed for this Standard from Geography, History, Naturkunde; and of a selection of more general pieces in prose and verse, which may have some bearing on the scientific subjects, or may simply alternate with them. Explanation of new ideas,

---
* A term used here in an exceptional sense.

sentences and expressions, laying stress on the sequence of ideas in the piece read.

2. *Grammar.* Further study of the simple Sentence; distinction of the different kinds of Pronouns, and complete knowledge of their inflections; Tenses of the Indicative Mood; Amplifications of Noun, Verb and Adjective, by means of words or phrases; knowledge of inflections of Adjectives, and use of principal Prepositions, on rules sharply defined, &c., as in the previous Standard.

Composition. Short descriptions and narratives, as in the previous year, as far as necessary from dictation by the teacher, but principally original paraphrase of matter read, or original composition on a descriptive, narrative or scientific subject previously learnt, or on some occurrence in the life of the pupil.

Sixth Standard.

1. *Reading and Explanation.* As in the two previous Standards, explanation of the scientific subjects of the year, from Geography, History, Naturkunde; also Poetry, specially selected.

2. *Grammar.* Complex sentences: Co-ordination and Subordination of Clauses; the remaining parts of the Verb; Conjunctions; all in sharply defined rules, &c., as in previous Standards.

3. *Composition.* Besides grammatical exercises, also various descriptions and narratives taken from the scientific subjects of the year; also short essays on persons discussed in class, and simple illustrations and arguments suggested by the reading lessons, and description of events from the child's life. Occasional attempts at letter-writing.

THE COMPLEMENTARY SCHOOL

consists of three (viz. 7th, 8th and 9th) Standards,[*] with advanced studies in Composition and Literature, which are not needed for our purpose.

[*] See p. 56.

STANDARDS FOR GEOGRAPHY.

AARGAU.

Fourth Class.

(In summer 1, in winter 2 hours, being part of the lessons on Language).

Descriptions of local scenes in the canton Aargau. Lessons in the art of reading maps. Tales from history of Switzerland. Descriptions of natural scenery of other countries.

Fifth, Sixth, Seventh and Eighth Classes.
(In summer 3, in winter 6 hours).

Fifth and Sixth Classes.
(a) Further practice in reading of maps.
(b) Repetition of descriptions of the canton Aargau.
(c) The geography of Switzerland.

Seventh and Eighth Classes.
(a) Repetition of the geography of Switzerland.
(b) Description of Europe and a synoptic view of the other quarters of the world.
(c) Outlines of Cosmography.

ALSACE-LORRAINE.

The lessons in Geography are intended to make the children acquainted with the whole earth as a dwelling-place for the human race; by the study of maps they are to acquire both tha ability to read its bearings and taste for continuing their geographical studies by independent effort after they have left school.

The first lessons in Geography treat of home in the narrowest sense. Subjects of study are: the house and the immediate neighbourhood; next, the district and the county. This expands into the study of Alsace-Lorraine and Germany; and these again are followed by the most important states of Europe, having regard to their peculiarities of territory and inhabitants. Lastly come the other quarters of the world according to their position and coast-lines, treating also of those natural and artificial productions which are most important in practical life.

The main facts of Mathematical Geography, principally the most obvious arguments in favour of the spherical shape of the Earth, her axial and orbital motions, so as to explain the phenomena of Day and Night and the Seasons, constitute the last year's study.

Based on Intuition, the teacher will explain the four Cardinal Points, and afterwards draw on the black-board a map of the native place and its immediate neighbourhood, so that the children may watch the gradual growth of the map. The signs used in these drawings must be explained and impressed by making the children copy these maps, especially the maps of local topography. Now the children will understand wall-maps, from which the several countries are to be studied, viz. their boundaries, relief and coast-lines. But from the outstart the study of each map must be enlivened by vivid descriptions of the peculiarities of the country and its inhabitants, partly given orally by the teacher and partly drawn from the Reading-book and from more elaborate books on Geography. After Europe has been studied, the children are to be taught from the globe the spherical shape of the earth, and are to be led to regard it as a cosmic body. The countries already studied must be once more examined on the globe, and then the other quarters of the world are studied from globe and maps combined. No Geography lesson is at any time to be given without the use of globe or map as means of intuition (Anschauungsmittel.) The lesson is to be impressed on the memory by questions and answers, and by utilizing (Verarbeitung) the Reading-book.

AUSTRIA.

General aim: Knowledge of the immediate home and of the Fatherland, physically, ethnographically and politically. The most important facts in the geography of Europe and the other quarters of the world, paying special attention to the relief of countries. Comprehension of the most obvious phenomena depending on the form, position and motion of the globe.

Third School Year. Knowledge of home, starting from the school-building. Explanation of the most important fundamental notions of Geography.

Fourth School Year. The native country.* Graphic representation of it on the black-board. General view of the Austro-Hungarian monarchy. Oral descriptions of countries and their inhabitants.

Fifth and Sixth School Years. The Austro-Hungarian monarchy. The globe. General view of the quarters of the world according to relief and coast-line. The earth as a cosmic body.

Seventh and Eighth School Years. Political geography of the

---

* The original is "Heimatland," for which a non-Austrian has hardly an equivalent: for a Bohemian child, Heimatland means Bohemia; for a Styrian, Styria, and so on. A composite empire like Austria, which is as yet only mechanically mixed—not, like England, chemically combined—has need of regulations and phraseologies hardly intelligible to homogeneous countries like Germany or France.

different quarters of the world. Descriptions of countries and populations.

Europe, specially central Europe. Detailed repetition and amplification of the Austro-Hungarian monarchy.

BAVARIA.

I. *Junior Classes.*

1. Land and Water: garden, meadow, field, forest, mountain, valley, wells, brook, river, pond, bog, lake, sea, &c. 2. Horizon and four Cardinal Points. 3. Differences of climate. 4. Situation of home.

II. *Intermediate Classes.*

1. Seas and Ocean. 2. Continents; Old and New World. 3. Quarters of the world. 4. Bavaria, geographical position of; cities, rivers, chief products, &c.

III. *Senior Classes.*

1. Germany; configuration; rivers, lakes, seas. 2. Europe; chief countries, capitals, chief rivers, &c.; peculiarities of the different nations; principal products of the chief countries of Europe, &c. 3. Practice in free-hand drawing of maps.

BELGIUM.

LOWER PRIMARY SCHOOLS.

First Stage (see p. 38).

First Year. 1. The four Cardinal Points. How to find your bearings from the position of the sun. Exercises.

2. Plans of the school-room and the school-building; (*a*) pupils are to read the plan; (*b*) pupils, 1st, are to draw its principal parts, and, 2nd, to mark the cardinal points on it.

3. First notions of geographical nomenclature given in walks and excursions.

Second Year. 1. The semi-cardinal and other intermediate points. Bearings (Orientation). Exercises.

2. Plans of the street, the neighbourhood and the parish: (*a*) reading of the plans; (*b*) pupils are, 1st, to draw the principal parts of each plan, and, 2nd, indicate the cardinal and intermediate points on it.

3. Lessons on the native place; geographical facts and nomenclature; natural productions; occupations of men, industry and commerce. Walks and excursions.

4. First idea of the canton.

5. Sensible horizon, shape of the earth; the earth as an unsupported body in space; earliest observations; familiar explanations.

6. Show on the globe, (*a*) Land and Sea, (*b*) the five quarters of the world and the great oceans.

7. Show on the globe Belgium and neighbouring countries.

Second Stage.

1. Exercises on the terrestrial globe. (*a*) Recapitulation of earliest notions (lessons on geometrical forms of the First Stage): centre, radius, diameter, great circles, smaller circles, hemispheres.

(*b*) New notions: axis, poles, meridians, equator, parallels, polar circles, tropics, zones.

2. Plans and charts. (*a*) Pupils to draw plans of the playground and of the street. Indicate bearings on these plans.

(*b*) Reading of a graduated series of Ordnance maps of the territory of the several districts (maps of the War Department specially prepared for elementary instruction).

(*c*) The canton; reading of the map.

(*d*) Pupils draw from memory sketches of the map of the parish and the canton. Study of distances.

3. Divisions of the globe: the five quarters of the world and the great oceans.

4. Boundaries of the five quarters of the world taught on the globe. Some great voyages described on the globe (e.g. that of Columbus or Maghellan, &c.), with the view of giving the pupils a familiar knowledge of the great divisions of the globe. The most important states of Europe and their capitals shown on maps and on the globe.

5. Belgium. (*a*) Boundaries, form, extent and population. Comparison with other countries.

(*b*) Explanation of the principal political terms: *commune, canton, arrondissement, province*, &c.

(*c*) Division of Belgium into provinces. Boundaries and capitals of each province.

(*d*) Outlines of Physical Geography. General aspect. Plains, mountains, hills, valleys and table-lands. Water-sheds, river-basins. Course of the Scheldt and of the Meuse, indicating the principal tributaries. Inhabitants and languages.

(*e*) Detailed description of the native province. Drawing from memory the map of the province and various other sketches.

Third Stage.

1. Recapitulation of the exercises on the terrestrial globe. Bearings ascertained by means of the mariner's compass and by observing the polar star. Latitude, Longitude. Position of a given point on the globe. Measuring of distances on the globe. Dimensions of the earth. Axial and orbital motions. Phases of the moon, eclipses and comets.

2. Exercises on Ordnance maps of the War Department. Practice in the use of the map of the town. Drawing of different sketches. Construction of map of the world. Projection.

3. Belgium. Recapitulation of the course of the Second Stage. Fuller study of its physical features. Animal, vegetable and mineral productions. Agricultural districts. Great centres of industry. Commerce; traffic by land and by water; ports; imports and exports.

Outline description of the nine provinces. Sketches and maps to be drawn from memory. Teach the pupils the use of "*The Official Guide for Travellers on Belgian Railways.*"*

4. Europe. Outline description of coast-lines, seas, gulfs, straits and large islands.

Principal countries of Europe: boundaries, governments, great cities, natural wealth, industry, commercial relations with Belgium.

5. Very succinct outlines of Asia, Africa, America and Polynesia. Some great voyages drawn in chalk on the black globe.†

6. Books on geography and travels read at home.

UPPER PRIMARY SCHOOLS.

1. Systematic recapitulation of the Mathematical Geography taught in the previous years.

The Solar System. The sun, planets, satellites. Comets, fixed stars, nebulæ, the Milky Way. Meteors, shooting stars, aerolites.

2. Maps. Charts of the War Department; projections, levelling, measurement of heights. Sketches and map-drawing.

3. Belgium. Recapitulation of the geography of Belgium; its agricultural, industrial and commercial geography.

4. Europe. Recapitulation of the previous course. Fuller study of its physical and political geography.

5. Outlines of the geography of Asia, Africa, America and Oceania. Great routes of navigation.

6. Private reading at home.

---

* "Bradshaw" studied at school !

† These black globes are admirable, and should be used in every school. THE COMPILER.

GENEVA.

Third Stage.

Conversations on Geography, principally on local Geography.

Fourth Stage (two lessons of three-quarters of an hour each per week.)

Detailed study of the parish. Geography of the canton of Geneva.

Fifth Stage (2 hours per week).

Definitions of geographical terms of Continents and Oceans: their relative positions, having special reference to Europe. (Very frequent use of the globe in the lessons.) Physical geography of Switzerland. Map-drawing.

Sixth Stage.

Political geography of Switzerland. Study of the neighbouring parts of France. General view of the five quarters of the world; Europe more in detail. The Earth,* her form and movements. Map-drawing. (Very frequent use in these lessons of the artificial globe.)

HAMBURG.†

Class III.—The children in this class are expected to acquire a knowledge of the immediate neighbourhood of their own homes, and to be able to understand a globe and a map.

Class IV.—An outline of the great divisions of the earth.

Class V.—Geography of Europe, with a particular knowledge of the geography of Germany.

Class VI.—Recapitulation and extension of the subject-matter taught in the previous years.

---

* In the fifth Stage the teacher is bidden to use the artificial globe, and yet it is not till the sixth Stage that the form of the earth is to be taught!

† Taken from the "Report on Schools in Germany and Switzerland," by George B. Davis, Clerk to the Birmingham School Board.

Class VII.—Particular knowledge of the geography of Germany, and of the most important foreign countries. Outlines of Mathematical Geography.

[The aim of these lessons is to give the pupils an elementary knowledge of Mathematical and Physical Geography, and a general knowledge of Political Geography, with more particular instruction in the countries of Europe, and especially of Germany; and also to make them acquainted with the countries and states in other parts of the world, according to their historical importance and their business relations to the countries of Europe.]

ITALY.

In the "Istruzioni e programmi per l'insegnamento della lingua italiana e dell' aritmetica nelle scuole elementari," I naturally do not find any course for Geography, but unfortunately these are the only Standards for Italian elementary schools sent me by the Italian Minister of Education.* Am I to infer from this that in the Italian elementary schools the course of instruction is restricted to the three R's ?

Happily I can give my readers an Italian course of Geography from the courses of study given in the Gymnasia and Lycea of Italy.

Geography of the first three classes in the Gynasium.—This study must be directed to a double purpose : first, to give to the students (and especially to those who will not attend the higher classes) an elementary but complete knowledge of the Earth, and particularly of Italy ; and, secondly, to be ancillary to the study of history.

That the knowledge of the Earth may be, albeit elementary, yet complete, it must comprise mathematical, astronomical, phy-

* My best thanks are due to the Italian Ministry for the cordial manner in which they have responded to my application.

sical and political Geography. But in all this, having regard to the nature of the science and to the tender age of the pupils, it is necessary that the professor should proceed with foresight in the selection of the matter to be taught, dwelling on principles, and illustrating them in such a manner as to render them clear to the intelligence of the students, taking care, however, that the popular explanations and illustrations which he makes use of do not militate against scientific explanations; and further, that he should not substitute some mere practical process for one thoroughly scientific, since frequently it is the case that, to understand or remember a fact better, it seems advantageous to communicate extrinsic facts, rather than to thoroughly investigate their intrinsic nature and their correlation to each other.

This premised, the study of Geography is divided as follows:

First Class. General notions of astronomical, topographical, physical and political Geography. Detailed geography of Italy.

Second Class. Geography of the Old World.

Third Class. Geography of America and Australia. Systematic recapitulation.

That the teaching may be easy, efficacious and most fruitful, it must be given vivâ voce, with no other help but the artificial globe and maps.

The student should imprint on his mind the form of the Earth, her parts and principal subdivisions and phenomena (accidenti), and the political arrangement in outline.

MUHLHAUSEN.

Fifth Class. Study of the geography and natural history of the parish, town, county, &c., keeping as nearly as may be abreast of the Reading-book, and starting from what the children know by direct observation.

Sixth Class. The special geography of Alsace, and the geography of Germany.

Seventh Class. In addition to repeating the lessons of the Sixth Class, there must be taught the essential parts of the geography of the countries bordering on Alsace, the figure and political divisions of Europe, and some knowledge of the other continents, especially North America.*

In Mathematical Geography, only the Earth's figure, divisions (zones, hemispheres) and rotation, together with the best known phenomena connected with these, and her place in the Solar System, are to be visualized.

NEUCHATEL.

Lower Grade.

First Year. Explanation by intuition of geographical terms, beginning with surrounding objects. Oral lessons on the terms, cardinal point, continent, isthmus, island, peninsula, plain, table-land, valley, mountain, city, town, village, hamlet. Also, ocean, sea, gulf, strait, channel, canal, lake, river, rivulet, source, bed, right and left banks, mouth, affluent, confluent, fall. General facts about continents and oceans. Preliminary explanation of maps of the country and canton, beginning with a map of the immediate neighbourhood drawn on the black-board by the master.

Second Year. Recapitulation of the foregoing, with expansions. General notions on the canton of Neuchâtel and on Switzerland.

Intermediate Grade.

First Year. Physical geography of Europe and Switzerland in its main outlines. That of the canton of Neuchâtel in detail.

---

* South-German emigrants mostly go to North America.

Second Year. Physical and political geography of Western Europe (British Isles, France, Belgium, Holland, Spanish peninsula, Italy) and of Switzerland.

Upper Grade.

First Year. 1. Geography, physical and political, of Central and Eastern Europe (Germany, Scandinavia and Denmark, Austria-Hungary, Balkan peninsula, Russia). Recapitulation of Switzerland. Asia, Australia. Drawing outlines of maps.

2. Sphere. The Earth; general notions given in oral lessons on its form; proofs of roundness; size as compared with moon and sun; circumference, distance from sun; rotation in twenty-four hours; day and night, axis, poles, equator, hemispheres, parallels, zones, meridians; continents, oceans; antipodes, horizon; motion through space in $365\frac{1}{4}$ days; seasons, months, weeks.

The Moon: her form, size and mean distance from Earth; her revolution round it; phases; rotation on axis; what is visible on her disc; eclipses; new and full moon; tides.

Second Year. 1. Geography. Recapitulation of Geography, physical and political, of Europe and Switzerland. America, Africa. Mapping.

N.B. It is earnestly recommended that in all the Grades the geographical features in the outline map should be filled in by the master. In the Upper Grade, the pupils will be required to reproduce such exercises.

2. Sphere. Earth and Moon; recapitulation of the last year's work. The Sun: size and distance from Earth; heat, light. Solar System. Fixed stars; the constellations.

Recapitulatory Course.

Geography. Recapitulation of the geography of Switzerland.

PRUSSIA.

1. AIM AND METHOD.

The instruction in Geography aims at making the children acquainted with their home, with their native land, with the German Empire and the chief countries of the earth. They are to be taught the globe, and about those heavenly bodies which stand in relationship to the earth. The instruction is to be essentially synthetic, and must be rendered visible by diagrams drawn on the black-board, by the terrestrial and celestial globes, and by maps.

2. STANDARDS.

Third Standard (2 hours). In this Standard the lessons begin by rendering clearly visible (zur Klaren Anschauung bringen) the most indispensable geographical notions by an accurate description of the school, the home and the district.

Fourth Standard (2 hours). Recapitulation and thorough mastery of the work of last Standard, followed by the study of Prussia.

Fifth Standard (2 hours). Recapitulation and expansion of the work of the last Standard; also detailed knowledge of the German Empire and general view of the other European states.

Sixth Standard (2 hours). Recapitulation and expansion of the work of the preceding Standard. · In addition to Prussia and Germany, the children will learn the geography of Austria and the other European countries. Of the other quarters of the world, the children will learn the chief countries and cities, mountain ranges and rivers, giving prominence to those countries which are distinguished historically, or by their commerce or civilization.

Mathematical Geography comprises:
  1. The Horizon.

2. Explanation of the most important points and circles on the globe.
3. Proofs of the spherical form of the Earth.
4. The Seasons and climatic Zones.
5. Fixed Stars.
6. The Sun and the Moon.
7. The Almanach.

SAXONY.

Introductory. All "Realien"* are based on preparatory lessons on Intuition, which are to be given in the first two years. In the Realien these lessons on Intuition have the additional object of training the children's power of observation, and, by means of intelligent and stimulating conversation, making them acquainted with many objects and phenomena, but principally with such as are taken from the child's immediate surroundings.†

The course of studies serves its purpose best if it adapts itself to the seasons.

A.—History.‡

---

* Realien (from *res*, thing) is a term indicating those studies which treat more of *things* than of *words* or abstract thought; hence the term comprises History, Geography, Chemistry, Natural History, Naturkunde, &c., but excludes Language and pure Mathematics.—THE COMPILER.

Foot-notes of the Original.

† . . . . (4) The teacher, proceeding by questions and answers, must insist upon it that the answers given be complete, and loudly and correctly pronounced. (5) In description, the teacher will avoid going too much into details. Intuitive teaching occupies itself exclusively with the facts occurring frequently in practical life, and which obtrude themselves of their own accord on the child's observation. (6) The description being finished, the class will recapitulate the whole lesson, at first with, and subsequently without, the object before them.

‡ Omitted with great regret, as not fitting into the plan of this volume. The different courses suggested are very admirable, and afford much food for reflection.—THE COMPILER.

B.—Geography.

The Geography lessons are intended to make the children intimately acquainted with Saxony and Germany; they are, moreover, to impart a general knowledge of the quarters of the world, especially of Europe, and the needful insight into the cosmic relationship of the Earth to other heavenly bodies.*

In schools with only two classes, Geography is not taught *in special lessons* till the fifth year, but in schools with three or more classes, Geography lessons, properly so called, begin in the third year.†

The course begins with the study of the immediate Home (Heimatkunde). By means of conversations on the house and the neighbourhood (all based on intuition), the teacher will establish the fundamental notions on Geography, and will teach the meaning and the reading of the map.‡

The courses of Geography proper will as a rule occupy two years.§

---

* Mathematical Geography is not to be made a separate branch in the simple elementary school (Volksschule), but is at all stages to be woven into the lessons on Physical and Political Geography in such a manner that, with an increased knowledge of the Earth's surface, the children should also form to themselves a clear picture of the relationship of the Earth in space to other heavenly bodies. Accordingly, mathematical Geography will treat of the form, size, position and motions of the Earth, of her relationship to the Sun and Moon, and of the phenomena due to these.

† There is a great deal of geographical knowledge imparted even to the lower classes by means of the lessons on Intuition.

‡ It is desirable that the teacher should make a simple map of the neighbourhood of each school; the children should learn to sketch a map of their own district from their own observation and measurements. It is less profitable to show a map ready-made than to draw it on the black-board in presence of the children, so that they should watch its gradual formation.

§ The teacher has the choice left him of about ten different courses of study; the Saxon Government insisting not so much on *what* you teach as on *how* you teach it. Saxony, admittedly in the van of the educational movement, occupies a position diametrically opposite to that of the English Government. The latter says to the teacher: Follow your own method; we do not inquire into

As indispensable means of instruction, it is unconditionally required that the school should possess a globe and wall-maps of Saxony, Germany and Europe. It is desirable that the pupils should have an atlas.

CANTON DE VAUD.

Lower Grade (about 2 years).

For the pupils of this stage, the lessons in Geography come under the head of lessons of observation and of conversation.

Cardinal Points. Topographical description. Principal edifices, squares, streets, roads, highways, indicating their direction, starting from the school-building; country-houses, hamlets, water-courses, mountains, &c.

Elementary study of the map of the parish. Explanations on the black-board of map-drawing, representing surfaces, distances and direction.

As this intuitive course is intended to serve as an introduction to the study of Geography, it must be utilized so as to impart to the pupils general notions of the science, taking special care to explain technical terms—e.g. in rivers: source, bed, right and left bank, mouth, tributary, waterfall, &c.

Intermediate Grade (2 to 3 years).

Continuation of the intuitive lessons of the Junior Classes, extending them to the topography of the district. Mountains, plains, water-courses, climate; natural productions; industries. Parishes and districts.

---

that; we examine results, and for these we pay. Saxony says: We insist on your following the best methods of teaching, such as are enjoined by the highest educational authorities; but you are the best judge as to what you can attempt with the material at your disposal. Logically, either position is defensible; but tested by ultimate Results, will anybody, comparing Saxony with England, maintain that hunting after, and payment by Results does yield the best Results?—THE COMPILER.

General study of the Canton de Vaud; then of Switzerland, principally in their physical aspect. Extent, boundaries, mountain-chains and their chief branches, table-lands, valleys, watercourses, lakes, climate, chief natural productions.

General study of the Hemispheres, if possible on the terrestrial globe. Poles, meridians, parallels, equator, tropics, polar circles. Division of the globe into two hemispheres and five continents. Oceans and their branches, seas, gulfs, straits. Shape and extent of continents, with their peninsulas and islands. Chief archipelagos and islands.

All these are to be taught in a general way, details being reserved for the next course.

Upper Grade (3 to 4 years).

Physical Geography of Europe. Boundaries, extent, oceans, seas, gulfs and straits. Islands and peninsulas, mountains, table-lands, plains, rivers and lakes. In the study of the different countries, instructions will be given on climate, productions of the soil, on vegetables and animals, as occasion offers.

Physical Geography of Asia, Africa, America and Polynesia. In this study the teacher will follow the order indicated in the study of Europe; but he will only dwell on main features, and will carefully avoid entering too much into details.

Political Geography of Europe. General facts on population. Different states. Populations, languages, religions, governments, climates, natural productions (mineral, vegetable and animal), industry and commerce. Capitals, cities, and remarkable localities.

Political Geography of other Continents, principally of those states which are commercially of greatest interest to us (United States, European Colonies).

Detailed study of Switzerland, physical and topographical. Political Geography. Statistics, history, manners, industries, religion and government.

Cosmography. Apparent movement of the celestial vault round the polar star. Apparent course of the sun and of the planets. Movements and phases of the moon. The Copernican system. Sun, centre of our system. Actual movement of the earth round the sun, and of the moon round the earth. Solar and lunar eclipses. Sizes and distances of the principal bodies of the solar system. Planets, comets, fixed stars. Elementary notions of gravitation.

ZURICH.

Introductory. The greater part of the lessons on the so-called "Realien"* have already been utilized as subject-matter for the different exercises in language, and especially as material for reading lessons. But just as it was insisted upon earlier, in determining the subject-matter for instruction, that in the hours of study of Language the reading lessons should be treated purely philologically, so now, on the other hand, it is distinctly demanded that these exercises in Language should not remain the sole aim, but that the reading lessons be regarded as a vehicle for imparting useful information,† and should be treated, as occasion requires, either as a summary of lessons formerly given, or as the starting-point of new subjects to be studied. These "realistic" lessons, then, are simply the continuation of the practices on Thinking and Speaking of the elementary school.

* On "Realien," see foot-note, p. 124.

† The countries that are leaders in education all agree that to utilize the reading lessons is a desirable means of impressing the memory, and also a great saving of time and expense, but not one of them requires that Geography, &c., in one word Realien, should be taught *throughout the year through reading lessons* only. (See New Code, § 19, C.) This is the only instance where the Department goes against the English maxim of not prescribing method.

Fourth Standard.
Realschule* (Intermediate Classes).
1. In continuation of the geographical studies begun in the lessons on observation in the earlier Standards (see p. 106), where the school-building and the immediate neighbourhood were used as a means for imparting the most important geographical notions exhibited on a map, the teacher will now, partly expanding the circle of direct observation (Anschauung), and partly by study of maps, aim at giving the children a graphic idea of the whole canton of Zürich, which shall be as complete and many-sided as possible, and include its several different regions. At the end of the course, the study of the relief of the canton is to serve as a preparation for a similar intuitive study (Betrachtung) of the whole of Switzerland.

Fifth Standard.

The geography of Switzerland is based all through on the study of the map: the direction of the different mountain-ranges and their ramifications; indication of the intervening valleys and their larger water-courses and lakes; description of the inhabitants of the different districts, and indication of the political boundaries and of most important statistics; description of individual cities and towns, and especially of such regions and localities as have any historic importance.

Sixth Standard.

Some account of the form of the Earth and of the geographical methods of indicating the situation of a given place on it; and then, on the basis of a general study of the distribution of land and water, a detailed description of Europe on the model of the study of the geography of Switzerland in the Fifth Standard.

The Complementary School consists of three classes, and continues the study of Geography so as to make a pretty complete course of study of it; but even in these three highest years a great deal of study is still devoted to Switzerland.

* A term used here in an exceptional sense.

A FEW FOREIGN TIME TABLES.

AARGAU.

Subjects.	Hours per week.							
	Summer.				Winter.			
	I. II.	III. IV.	V. VI.	VII. VIII.	I. II.	III. IV.	V. VI.	VII. VIII.
1. Religion	2	2	2	2	2	2	2	2
2. Language	9	7	5	3	10	12	7	7
3. Realien* (i.e. History, Geography, Sciences)	—	—	3	3	—	—	6	6
4. Arithmetic and Mensuration	3	2	2	3	4	4	4	4
5. Drawing	—	1	1	—	—	2	1	1
6. Writing	—	2	1	1	—	2	2	2
7. Singing	1	1	1	1	1	2	2	2
8. Gymnastics	2	2	2	2	2	2	2	2
	17	17	17	14	19	26	26	26

* See foot-note, p. 124.

AUSTRIA.

Time Table for an Elementary School of six Standards (sechsclassige Volksschule).

In Elementary School with six Classes, the 1st, 2nd, 3rd and 4th Class occupy each one year. The 5th and 6th Classes subdivide themselves into two sections each, thus: 5th Class—1st section, the 5th school year; 2nd section, the 6th school year. 6th Class—1st section, the 7th school year; 2nd section, the 8th school year.

Subjects	1st Class 1st School yr	2nd Class 2nd School yr	3rd Class 3rd School yr	4th Class 4th School yr	5th Class Section 1 5th School yr	5th Class Section 2 6th School yr	6th Class Section 1 7th School yr	6th Class Section 2 8th School yr
Religion	1	1	2	2	2	2	2	2
Mother-tongue	12	10	9	9	6	6	6	6
Arithmetic	6½	4	4*	4*	4*	4*	4*	4*
Naturkunde‖	—	—	1	1	4	4	4	4
Geography and History	—	—	1	2	4†	4†	4†	4†
Writing	—	2	2	2	1	1	1	1
Drawing, Free-hand and Geometrical	2½	2½	2½	2	3	3	4†	4†
Singing	2½	2½	2½	2½	2½	2½	2½	2½
Gymnastics	2½	2½	2	2	2	2	2§	2§
Needlework	—	—	3	3	3	3	4	4
Total number of hours per week: For Boys	18	20	23	25	27	27	28	28
" Girls	18	20	25	27	28	28	28	28

* For Girls, 3 hours.   † For Girls, 3 hours.   ‡ For Girls, 2 hours.   § For Girls, 1 hour.

‖ Naturkunde subdivides itself in the Fifth and Sixth Classes into Naturgeschichte (Natural History) and Naturlehre (Physics), two hours per week being given to each.

BELGIUM.

TABLE A.—PRIMARY SCHOOLS.

	First or Elementary Grade.		Second Grade.		Third Grade.	
	Schools for		Schools for		Schools for	
I. Compulsory Subjects for all the Schools.	Boys.	Girls.	Boys.	Girls.	Boys.	Girls.
Morals, Reading, Mother-tongue } Writing	11 4	10 3	6 2	6 2	6 1	6 1
Arithmetic and Metric System	2	2	4	3	4	3
Drawing and Geometrical Designs	2	1	3	2	3	3
Geography, History	1	1	3	2	3	2
Natural Sciences	1	1	1	1	1	2
Gymnastics	1	1	1	1	2	1
Singing	—	3	—	4	—	4
Needlework						
II. Optional Subjects.						
A foreign tongue (seconde langue)	3	3	5	5	5	5
	25	25	28	28	28	28

BELGIUM.

Table B.—Upper Primary Schools.

Subjects.	Boys' Schools.	Girls' Schools.
Morals and Reading	2	2
Writing	1	1
Mother-tongue	4	4
Additional Language (seconde langue)	5	5
Arithmetic	3	3
Drawing and Practical Geometry	3	2
Geography	1	1
History	1	1
Political Economy and Constitutional Law	1	—
Notions on Natural Science, Hygiene, Agriculture, Horticulture and Arboriculture	4	3
Book-keeping	1	1
Gymnastics	2	1
Vocal Music	2	1
Needlework and Domestic Economy	—	5
	30	30

Seen and annexed to our Decree, dated 20th July, 1880.

(Signed) The Minister of Public Instruction, P. Van Humbeck.

NEUCHATEL.

Subjects.	Lower Grade. 1st yr. B. FIXED	Lower Grade. 1st yr. G. FIXED	Lower Grade. 2nd year. B. MIN.	Lower Grade. 2nd year. B. MAX.	Lower Grade. 2nd year. G. MIN.	Lower Grade. 2nd year. G. MAX.	Intermediate Grade. 1st year. B. MIN.	Intermediate Grade. 1st year. B. MAX.	Intermediate Grade. 1st year. G. MIN.	Intermediate Grade. 1st year. G. MAX.	Intermediate Grade. 2nd year. B. MIN.	Intermediate Grade. 2nd year. B. MAX.	Intermediate Grade. 2nd year. G. MIN.	Intermediate Grade. 2nd year. G. MAX.	Upper Grade. 1st year. B. MIN.	Upper Grade. 1st year. B. MAX.	Upper Grade. 1st year. G. MIN.	Upper Grade. 1st year. G. MAX.	Upper Grade. 2nd year. B. MIN.	Upper Grade. 2nd year. B. MAX.	Upper Grade. 2nd year. G. MIN.	Upper Grade. 2nd year. G. MAX.	Course of Repetition. B.	Course of Repetition. G.
1. French Language :																								
1. Reading and Recitation	5	4	5	5	4	4	4	5	3	3	4	5	3	3	3	4	2	3	3	4	2	3	2	2
2 & 4. Vocabulary, Elocution, Composition	4	3	4	4	3	3	4	4	3	3	4	4	3	3	3	4	2	3	3	4	2	3	1	1
3. Grammar, Orthography and Analysis	4	4	4	5	4	5	4	5	4	5	4	5	4	5	4	5	3	5	4	5	3	5	1½	1½
2. Writing	3	3	2½	2½	2½	2½	2	2½	2	2	2	2	2	2	1	2	1	2	1	2	1	2	½	½
3. Arithmetic :																								
1. Mental Arithmetic	1	1	1	1	1	1	1	1	1	1	1	1	1	1	1	1	1	1	1	1	1	1	½	½
2 & 3. Theory and Practice	4	4	4	5	4	5	4	5	4	5	4	5	4	5	4	5	4	5	3½	4½	4	5	1	1
4. Book-keeping	...	...	...	...	...	...	...	...	...	...	...	...	...	...	½	½	½	½	½	½	½	½	½	½
4. Geography, simply	1	1	1½	1½	1½	1½	2	2	2	2	2	2	2	2	...	...	...	...	...	...	...	...	½	½
Ditto, with Globe	...	...	...	...	...	...	...	...	...	...	...	...	...	...	2	2½	2	2	2	2½	2	2	...	...
5. History :																								
1. National History	...	...	...	...	...	...	1	1½	1	1	1	2	1	1	1	1	1	1	1	1	1	1	½	½
2. Universal History	...	...	...	...	...	...	...	...	...	...	...	...	...	...	½	1	½	½	½	1	½	½	...	...
6. Singing	1	1	1	1	1	1	1	1	1	1	1	1	1	1	1	1	1	1	1	1	1	1	...	...
7. Drawing	1	1	1	1	1	1	1	1	1	1	1	1	1	1	2	2	2	2	2	2	2	2	1½	...
8. Elements of Geometry and of Mensuration	...	...	...	...	...	...	...	...	...	...	...	...	...	...	½	½	...	...	1	1	...	...	...	...
9. Elementary notions on Natural Science or on Agriculture*																								
10. Gymnastics†	...	...	...	...	...	...	...	...	...	...	...	...	...	...	...	...	...	...	...	...	...	...	...	...
11. Constitutional Law (instruction civique)	...	...	...	...	...	...	...	...	...	...	...	...	...	...	½	½	...	...	½	½	...	...	½	...
Domestic Economy and Needlework	...	2	...	...	2	2	...	...	2	4	...	...	2	4	...	...	4	4	...	...	4	4	...	2
	24	24	24	26	24	26	24	28	24	28	24	28	24	28	24	30	24	30	24	30	24	30	10	10

* No special hours fixed.

† Lessons on Gymnastics are not counted in the hours of maxima and minima of the Courses of Study; in the Lower Grade they are given in the intervals of study and during recreation; from nine years of age and upwards, the boys must be classified according to age, in accordance with the Federal enactment of the 13th Sept. 1878; from nine to twelve, they will have two lessons per week of one hour each; from twelve to fifteen, the number of hours may be reduced to one and a half. For the girls, one hour of Gymnastics a week is sufficient.

PRUSSIA.

Subjects.	Standards I. and II.	Standards III. and IV.	Standard V.	Standard VI.
Religion	4	4	4	4
German	11	8	8	8
Arithmetic	4	4	4	4
Geometry	—	—	—	2
Drawing	—	2	2	2
"Realien"* (i.e. Geography, History, Science, &c.)	—	6	8	8
Singing	1	2	2	2
Gymnastics for Boys } Needlework for Girls }	2	2	2	2
	22	28	30	32

* See foot-note, p. 124.

ENGLISH STANDARDS AND STAGES.

I.—STANDARDS.

First Standard.

Reading. To read a short paragraph from a book, not confined to words of one syllable.*

Writing. Copy in manuscript character a line of print, on slates or in copy-books, at choice of managers; and write from dictation a few common words.

Arithmetic. Notation and numeration up to 1000. Simple addition and subtraction of numbers of not more than four figures, and the multiplication-table to 6 times 12.

Second Standard.

Reading. To read a short paragraph from an elementary reading book.

Writing. A sentence from the same book, slowly read once, and then dictated. Copy-books (large or half-text) to be shown.

Arithmetic. Notation and numeration up to 100,000. The four simple rules to short division (inclusive).

†*Grammar.* To point out the nouns and verbs in the passages read or written.

Third Standard.

Reading. To read a short paragraph from a more advanced reading-book.

---

* English words should, for teaching purposes, be classified according to regularity or irregularity of structure, and not at all according to number of syllables.—THE COMPILER.

† Optional.

Writing. A sentence slowly read out once, and then dictated from the same book. Copy-books to be shown (small-hand, capital letters and figures).

Arithmetic. Notation and numeration up to 1,000,000. Long division and compound addition and subtraction (money).

*Grammar. *To point out the nouns, verbs, adjectives, adverbs and personal pronouns.*

Fourth Standard.

Reading. To read a few lines of prose or poetry selected by the Inspector.

Writing. Eight lines slowly read out once, and then dictated from a reading-book. Copy-books to be shown (improved small-hand).

Arithmetic. Compound rules (money) and reduction (common weights and measures).

*Grammar. *Parsing of a simple sentence.*

Fifth Standard.

Reading. Improved reading.

Writing. Writing from memory the substance of a short story read out twice; spelling, grammar and handwriting to be considered.

N.B. An exercise in dictation may, at the discretion of the Inspector, be given in place of the above.

Arithmetic. Practice, bills of parcels and simple proportion.

*Grammar. *Parsing, with analysis of a "simple" sentence.*

Sixth Standard.

Reading. Improved reading.

Writing. A short theme or letter; the composition, spelling, grammar and handwriting to be considered.

N.B. Same as Fifth Standard.

Arithmetic. Proportion, vulgar and decimal fractions.

*Grammar. *Parsing and analysis of a short "complex" sentence.*

* Optional.

N.B. As to the words printed in italics, see Article 19, C. 2. For other class subjects (to be arranged with the Inspector), see Article 19, C. 1.

Art. 19, C. 1. The sum of 2s. (*or* 4s.) per scholar, according to the average number of children, above 7 years of age, in attendance throughout the year (Article 26), if *the classes* from which the children are examined above Standard I. pass a creditable examination in any one (*or two*) of such definite subjects of instruction as are shown by the time-table to have been taught throughout the year *through reading lessons*, illustrated, if necessary, by maps, diagrams, specimens, &c., and according to a graduated scheme which the Inspector reports to be well adapted to the capacity of the children.

2. Grammar and plain needlework may be taken as subjects under this paragraph (C.). The extent of the examination in grammar is indicated by the passages printed in italics in Article 28. The examination in needlework will be conducted according to the Third Schedule, and will extend to the girls presented in Standard I.

COMMENTS ON STANDARDS OF ARITHMETIC.

First Standard.

Numeration up to 1000 is difficult for young children, and is useless until some clear idea of the meaning of smaller numbers has been acquired; but no analysis of numbers or other mode of giving such clear idea is insisted on. Children are thus forced into knowledge for which their minds are insufficiently developed.

Continental Codes wisely confine their First Standard to "the Four Rules applied to numbers 1 to 12 or 1 to 20," as children of such tender years cannot possibly attach any idea to those useless big numbers.

Again: With us, Addition and Subtraction are required up to 9999, while Numeration is only required up to 1000, the symbols being thus used *before* instead of *after* the realistic conception of the things symbolized.

Second Standard.

The exaction of Long Multiplication at this early stage necessitates Numeration up to 100,000; thus numbers have to be dealt with, which aggravate the evils of the First Standard. It is not immediately obvious that 100,000 affords a rational halting-place.

Third Standard.

At length, after having mastered the complicated and difficult rules of Long Multiplication and Long Division, the child is taught the far easier rules of Addition and Subtraction of Money. For those large abstract numbers, of which it is difficult for a child to form an adequate conception, are substituted the familiar units of every-day life. The fundamental maxim of good teaching, that the Concrete should precede the Abstract, is reversed; and it is not till after going through a long course of complicated work, the bearing of which must appear a complete mystery, that the child is taught the rules which are of all others the most useful in the affairs of life; rules, too, which give little difficulty when taught simultaneously with addition and subtraction of units, tens and hundreds. The principle of "carriage" is far more easily understood when applied to money than to abstract quantities.

Fourth Standard.

This Standard is a mere waste of a year. If the Four Rules have been taught rationally, concrete and abstract quantities advancing together, the application of the rules to different weights and measures requires but little teaching and short practice, especially if the child is allowed to consult the tables, as he ought to be.

Fifth Standard.

Although easy questions in Simple Practice can be worked without a knowledge of any but Aliquot Fractions, Compound

Practice (and even Simple. Practice if there is a fraction in the number of articles given) requires a knowledge of Fractions.

Bills of Parcels being merely a mode of arranging a number of multiplications and adding the products, should not be dignified as a separate rule; in many cases, too, Fractions are required.

Simple Proportion is unintelligible without a knowledge of Fractions: Proportion is the Equality of Ratios; a Ratio is an Abstract Fraction; and yet even Concrete Fractions are relegated to Standard VI.

To the contention that the so-called Proportion sums may be worked by the Unitary Method, the rejoinder is obvious that even the Unitary Method requires a knowledge of Fractions.

Sixth Standard.

Here, again, Proportion is placed before Fractions, from which alone its fundamental idea is derived. Standards IV. and V. dealt with too small a field, so that Vulgar and Decimal Fractions, with all that they include, have to be crowded into one Standard, which thus errs in the opposite direction, though even now the course is left incomplete. No mention is made of what is the most instructive or "formative" portion of the whole subject, namely, Properties of Numbers (such as Even and Odd, Prime and Composite Numbers, Measures and Multiples, Divisibility of Numbers, &c.). There is no allusion made to Interest, Discount, Stocks, or Evolution.

The subjects to be learned are crowded together at the beginning and at the end, while the course is attenuated in the middle. If children were confined in the early Standards to numbers within their grasp; if at each stage the Concrete were made to precede the Abstract; if money operations were taught simultaneously with simple rules; if Fractions, which are so useful in common life, and afford such a suitable field for training the reasoning powers, were introduced in different stages as soon as possible,—a great deal more ground could be covered, and that more profitably too, in the same time; and from first to last the bearing of their studies upon the world around them would be evident to the children's own minds.

Mental Arithmetic, a most important discipline, and really the basis of all Written Arithmetic, is only vaguely mentioned in a foot-note.

Comments on Standards of Grammar.

The whole spirit of the teaching suggested by the Standards is faulty. Children begin with the Parts of Speech, for which no need has been shown, instead of beginning with analysis of Simple Sentences, which would suggest the necessity for naming the words performing certain functions. The symbols are here also taught before the things symbolized, and thus the subject loses its chief value as an instrument of Education.

Again, Composition is only demanded in the two highest Standards, which few of our children attain to; but if Analysis were introduced early, Composition, which is its correlative, might advance pari passu with it.

II.—STAGES.

First Stage.

English Literature. Two hundred lines of poetry, got by heart, with knowledge of meaning and allusions. Writing a letter on a simple subject.

N.B. This Stage may be taken only with Standard IV.

Mathematics. Algebra, notation, addition, subtraction, Euclid, Book I. prop. 1 to 15 inclusive.

Latin. Grammar to the end of regular verbs.

French. Grammar to end of regular verbs. Ten pages of a French vocabulary.

German. Grammar, to end of regular verbs. Ten pages of a German vocabulary.

Physical Geography. The nature of a river or stream, whence it is supplied, and what becomes of it. Evaporation and condensation. Rain, snow, and hail, dew and mist. The atmosphere and its composition. Winds. An explanation of the terms river-basin, and water-shed. The boundaries of the great river-basins of England.

Second Stage.

English Literature. Two hundred and fifty lines of poetry, not before brought up, repeated; with knowledge of meaning and allusions. Writing a paraphrase of a passage of easy prose.

N.B. This Stage may be taken only with Standard IV. or V.

Mathematics. Algebra, to simple equations (inclusive). Euclid, Book I.

Latin. Irregular verbs and first rules of syntax. Knowledge of Delectus or other first Latin reading-book. Translation of simple sentences of English (three or four words) into Latin.

French. Grammar, and translation into English of easy narrative sentences. Ten pages of a French conversation book approved by Inspector.

German. Grammar, and translation into English of easy narrative sentences. Ten pages of a German conversation book approved by Inspector.

Physical Geography. The ocean, its extent and divisions, depth, saltness and currents. Action of waves. Sea beaches. The phenomena of the tides.

Third Stage.

English Literature. Three hundred lines of poetry, not before brought up, repeated with knowledge of meaning and allusions. Writing a letter or statement, the heads of the topics to be given by the Inspector.

Mathematics. Algebra, to quadratic equations (inclusive). Euclid, Books I. and II. Elements of mensuration.

Latin. The Latin Grammar. Cæsar de Bello Gallico, Book I. Somewhat longer sentences to be translated from English into Latin.

French. Grammar and knowledge of some easy French book approved by Inspector. Translation of conversational sentences into French. Tolerable correctness of pronunciation.

German. Grammar, and knowledge of some easy German book approved by Inspector. Translation of conversational sentences into German. Tolerable correctness of pronunciation.

Physical Geography. Form and size of the earth, and its motions. Day and night. The seasons of the year; how they depend upon the relative positions of the earth and sun. Moon's dimensions and distance; explanation of her phases. General arrangement of the planetary system.

COMMENTS ON PHYSICAL GEOGRAPHY.

It is difficult to criticize these Stages seriously : Mathematical and Physical Geography are jumbled together, and the sequence of subjects could hardly be more unmanageable for a teacher if it had been arranged by chance. Beyond the pious aspiration that good books may be forthcoming, implied in Article 19 C. 1, no reliable provision is made for the earliest notions; such as the Cardinal Points, reading a Map, Longitude and Latitude, &c. No knowledge is required of the general character of the great continents, of the ranges of mountains, the river systems, countries, their climates and productions. The Winds are treated of in an earlier Standard than the Rotation of the Earth, without which no winds except the Land and Sea Breezes can be understood; and the Tides before the Motion of the Moon. The subjects of the first stage are of a character for the comprehension of which there has been no previous training.

COMMENTS ON GEOMETRY.

The objection to this Standard is, that the teacher is compelled to follow the sequence of Euclid. It is disputed that this is the best method for children, who are not likely to carry the subject further, but at any rate an alternative should be allowed to those teachers who prefer the Modern Geometry.

The Standards of Languages may profitably be compared with those of Belgium; and "English Literature" so called seems really below all comment.

MEMORIAL OF THE CONFERENCE ON CODE REFORM.

To the President, Vice-President, and Lords of the Committee of Council on Education.

We, the undersigned, being intimately associated with educational work in this country, and convinced that the whole range of Education from the Elementary School to the Universities is so organically connected, that the course of instruction followed in the Elementary Schools cannot but affect directly the work of the Secondary Schools, and through them, to an increasing extent, even the Universities, have long felt that the educational provisions of the existing Code fail to secure either a solid foundation for all Education, or the substantial equipment of the children passing through the public Elementary Schools for their future duties and responsibilities.

We have accordingly heard with the utmost satisfaction that your Lordships have under contemplation the making of fundamental changes in the Regulations of the Code.

We would respectfully submit—

That the experience of the past has led to the acceptance of certain general Principles of Education, and that these cannot be neglected without seriously detracting from the value of the early training given at school.

The most important of these principles are—
- 1st. That the Course of Studies should, at each stage, be in harmony with, and adapted to, the natural development of the child's mind and body.
- 2nd. That all teaching should proceed from the Known to the Unknown; from the Particular and the Concrete to the General and the Abstract; and from the Empirical to the Rational and Scientific.

We would respectfully urge that the Standards (Art. 28) and Stages (Schedule IV.) are, at different points, at variance with one or other of these principles.

We would remind your Lordships that these principles were enunciated by the Committee of Council thirty-seven years ago, and embodied in the Minutes on Methods of Teaching issued by the Committee in 1844; and we would also point out that they are recognized in a greater or less degree in the most approved Manuals of Method now in the hands of those who are being trained as Elementary Teachers.

We would therefore ask for the unreserved adoption of these principles as the basis of our Public Elementary Education; and respectfully submit to the consideration of your Lordships the Standards of Examination which are appended to this Memorial, these being, in our belief, in closer general agreement with the educational principles enunciated above than those at present in operation.

(*Signed*)

JOHN W. CALDICOTT, D.D., Oxon, Head Master of the Grammar School, Bristol; Vice-Chairman of the Bristol School Board.

CHARLES DONCASTER, Chairman, School Management Committee, Sheffield School Board.

H. W. EVE, M.A., Head Master of University College School, London; late Fellow of Trinity College, Cambridge.

GEORGE CAREY FOSTER, B.A., F.R.S., F.C.P., Fellow of, and Professor of Physics in, University College, London.

J. H. GLADSTONE, F.R.S., Member of London School Board.

JAMES HANSON, Chairman, School Management Committee, Bradford School Board.

P. HENRICI, Ph.D., F.R.S., Professor of Applied Mathematics in University College, London.

J. F. McCALLAN, M.A., Vicar of New Basford, and Chairman, School Management Committee, Nottingham School Board.

E. F. M. MacCARTHY, M.A., Head Master of King Edward VI.'s Middle School, Birmingham; Vice-Chairman, and Chairman of the Education Committee, Birmingham School Board.

J. M. D. MEIKLEJOHN, M.A., Professor of the Theory, History and Practice of Education in the University of St. Andrew's, Scotland.

RICHARD MORRIS, M.A., LL.D., Ex-President of the Philological Society, London.

T. D. C. MORSE, Member of the London School Board; formerly a Diocesan Inspector of Schools in the Diocese of Salisbury; sometime Lecturer in Latin and History at Queen's College, Harley Street.

F. MAX MÜLLER, M.A., Professor of Comparative Philology at Oxford.

J. ALLANSON PICTON, M.A. (Lond. Un.), late Member of the London School Board.

A. SONNENSCHEIN, Teacher.

MARK WHITWILL, Chairman of the School Board for Bristol.

MARK WILKS, Chairman, School Management Committee, London School Board.

JOSEPH WOOD, Chairman of Leicester School Board.

RICHARD WORMELL, D.Sc., M.A., Head Master of the School of the Corporation for Middle Class Education in the Metropolis.

WM. BARNES, M.A., LL.D., Chairman, Education and School Management Committee, Leeds School Board (signs Memorial, omitting the latter sentence of last paragraph, and Appendices).

PROPOSED STANDARDS OF EXAMINATION.

Infant Standard (for last year of Infant School).

Reading and Writing.*

Arithmetic.

The elementary arithmetic of the numbers 1 to 12 worked mentally, viz.

(a) Counting forwards and backwards.
(b) Even and odd.
(c) Counting by intervals.
(d) The four Rules.

N.B.—All lessons to be based upon concrete quantities.

Geography.

Relative position of objects to be marked on slates or paper.

Plan of *school-room* drawn to scale from measurements taken by children. Understanding of it to be tested by requiring children to mark on the plan the positions of chairs, &c., also to place such objects in the room as marked on plan.

Cardinal points of the compass.

First Standard.

Reading.

To read with perception of meaning sentences of easy and fairly regular notation; subject-matter to be within the capacity of children between 7 and 8.

---

* Division of spoken sentence into words and syllables (orally). Letters and Arabic and Roman figures derived from lessons on form; the writing of such letters and figures connected with drawing as taught in the Kindergarten. The Standards imply a previous preparation in the Infant School, which should include the following, viz. training of the power of perception and that of expression, such as is aimed at in the Kindergarten system; e.g. to see and hear quickly and correctly, shapes, colours, relative positions, relative sizes of various objects interesting to children; to answer on the above readily and clearly, in complete phrases, *not mere Yes and No.*

Writing.

To write in a round hand short childish sentences in answer to simple questions.

To write from dictation, or copy from print, words, phrases, &c., within the range of the children's thoughts.

Spelling, except of words of regular notation, not to count in examinations.

Arithmetic.

(*a*) Counting up to 100, forwards and backwards.

(*b*) Counting by intervals of 10, 2, 3, 4 and 5 up to 100.

(*c*) Notation and numeration (the latter oral) of numbers up to 100; including breaking up into tens and units, e.g. 37 is to be explained as three tens and seven ones; and 50 as 5 tens and no ones.

(*d*) Simple addition within the same limits.

(*e*) Addition (mentally) of two money items whose sum does not exceed a shilling; and subtraction (mentally) where the minuend does not exceed a shilling.

Geography. (Same as Infant Standard.)

Second Standard.

Reading.

To read anything that is intelligible to average children of 8 to 9. Apprehension of meaning always required.

Writing.

To show copy-books (large half-text).

To write in a fair round hand, from dictation, easy sentences from any book interesting to young children.

Correct spelling expected, except in very anomalous words.

Arithmetic.

(*a*) Notation and numeration up to 1000.

(*b*) Counting by intervals of 6, 7, 8 and 9 up to 100.

(*c*) The pence table, and the multiplication table to 6 times 12.

(*d*) Addition and subtraction (simple and money within the same limits).

(e) Multiplication with multiplier of one digit where the product does not exceed 1000 or £1000.

(f) Short division with divisor not exceeding 6, and dividend not exceeding 1000 or £1000.

(g) Arithmetic (mental) of half-a-crown.

Grammar and Recitation.

To answer in complete sentences with good enunciation and with grammatical correctness.

Recitation, with distinct utterance and sense of meaning, of a few suitable verses taught orally.

Division of sentence into subject and predicate; distinction of verbs from nouns or adjectives (action-words from name-words).

Geography.

The home or school-house, with neighbouring streets or fields. Plans or map of one or more of these drawn roughly from measurements taken by the children.

Finding the positions on floor of school-room of points marked on plan, and conversely.

Meaning of maps.

Cardinal points of the compass.

A special knowledge of the district in which the school is situated, studied from a map of the locality.

English History.

Stories and Biographies before the Norman Conquest, illustrative of, e.g., the English Conquest, the introduction of Christianity, invasion of the Danes, Alfred the Great, Canute, Harold.

Reading. *Third Standard.*

To read prose with animation, or poetry with expression and sense of rhythm.

Writing.

To show copy-books (small-hand, &c.).

To write from dictation with correct spelling, and proper punctuation.

Arithmetic.

(*a*) Notation and numeration.
(*b*) The multiplication table to 12 times 12.
(*c*) The four Rules (simple and money).
(*d*) The arithmetic (mental) of a pound, involving a knowledge of such simple aliquot parts as $\frac{1}{2}, \frac{1}{4}, \frac{1}{8}, \frac{1}{10}, \frac{1}{5}$.

Grammar and Recitation.

To answer, &c. &c., and with increased intelligence.

Recitation—verse—with good enunciation.

Variety of modes in which subject and predicate may be made up. Inflection of nouns, adjectives and verbs.

Geography.

Special knowledge of the Geography of the county in which the school is situated, with the physical features of the locality.

General knowledge of the Geography of England and Wales, including coast-lines, directions of chief mountain ranges and rivers; river-basins; with towns above 50,000 inhabitants.

Explanation of geographical terms necessarily occurring in connection with the above subjects.

The above to be learnt from an outline physical map, without division into counties.

English History.

Stories and Biographies from the Norman Conquest to 1485, e.g. Hereward, Becket, Richard I. and the Crusades, John and Magna Charta, Simon de Montfort and House of Commons, Edward I., Edward III. and Black Prince, Wat Tyler, Henry V., Joan of Arc, Warwick and the Wars of the Roses, Caxton.

Reading.   *Fourth Standard.*

To read with intelligence, from a standard modern book or from the day's paper, some incident or easy narrative.

Writing.

To show copy-books, &c.

To write from dictation with complete punctuation, &c. The piece to be more difficult than in the previous Standard.

Arithmetic.

(a) Compound Rules and Reduction (money, common weights and measures).

[Scholars may be allowed to consult the Tables of Weights and Measures.]

(b) Easy per-centages, viz. 5 per cent. and $2\frac{1}{2}$ per cent.

(c) Fractions (1) of aliquot parts, not smaller than $\frac{1}{10}$, of sums of money leaving no remainder. (2) Multiples of aliquot parts of ditto (proper fractions only).

(d) Factors, measures and multiples.

Grammar, Recitation, and English Literature.

To answer, &c. &c., and with increased intelligence.

Recitation of prose or verse from standard authors.

Inflection, &c., of pronouns, remaining parts of speech, parsing.

Geography.

Outlines of the Geography of Great Britain and Ireland, Physical and Political, including division into counties. Towns of above 20,000 inhabitants, or of historical importance. Chief coal-fields and industries of the country, with special attention to the principal trade of the district where the school is situated.

Figure of the Earth shown from familiar facts.

Explanation of geographical terms necessarily occurring in connection with the above subjects.

English History.

Stories and Biographies from 1485 to 1688, e.g. Henry VIII., More, Surrey, Cranmer, Protector Somerset, Queen Elizabeth, Mary Queen of Scots, Sidney, Raleigh, Drake, Shakspeare, Bacon, Charles I., Prince Rupert, Cromwell, Blake, Milton, Newton, Claverhouse, James II.

Fifth Standard.

Reading.

To read with intelligence from some approved authors of the last century.

Writing.

To write from memory the substance of a short story read out twice; spelling, grammar, and handwriting to be considered.

Arithmetic.

(*a*) Proper fractions, improper fractions, and mixed numbers; interconversion of the two latter.

(*b*) Addition and subtraction of fractions of the same denomination.

(*c*) Multiplication and division of fractions by integers.

(*d*) Finding common measures by inspection.

(*e*) Reduction of fractions to lowest terms.

(*f*) Simple practice and household accounts.

Grammar, Recitation, and English Literature.

More than mere answers; signs of ability to converse.

Dramatic recitation.

Parsing.   Analysis of simple sentences.

Geography.

Chief divisions of land and water on the globe: continents and oceans.

Outlines of the Geography of Europe, Physical and Political.

Instances of the influence exerted by the physical features of a country on the distribution of population and on their industrial pursuits.

Day and night due to the earth's rotation.

Explanation of terms necessarily occurring in connection with the above subjects.

English History.

The general History from 1066 to 1688, with reference to its Social, Political, Literary, and Religious features.

Reading.   *Sixth Standard.*

To read with intelligence from approved authors of the Elizabethan period and 17th century.

Writing.

To write a short business letter.

Arithmetic.

(*a*) Complete division of integers, giving the quotient as an integer, a mixed number, or a proper fraction.

(*b*) Simplification of compound fractions, and multiplication and division of fractions.

(*c*) Least common multiple.

(*d*) Addition and subtraction of fractions.

(*e*) Solution of problems by the method known as the "Unitary Method."

(*f*) Simplification of complex fractions.

Grammar, Recitation, and English Literature.

To tell a short story.

To describe some feature of the neighbourhood as the beginning of a short conversation.

Dramatic recitation.

Parsing. Correction of common errors. Analysis of complex sentences.

Geography.

Outlines of the Geography of the World, with especial reference to the British Colonies and their commerce.

Motion of the earth round the sun: causes of the Seasons, and of the main differences of climate on the globe. Distribution of the more important types of Animal and Vegetable Life as affected by zones of climate.

Explanation of terms necessarily occurring in connection with the above subjects.

English History.

The general History from 1688 to 1832, with reference to its Social, Political, Literary and Religious features.

Reading. *Seventh Standard.*

To read with intelligence a passage from Chaucer.

Writing.
To write a short essay.

Arithmetic.
(*a*) Notation and numeration from 1,000,000 to ·000,001.
(*b*) Conversion of vulgar fractions to decimals and vice versâ.
(*c*) The four Rules in decimals.
(*d*) Approximate calculations.
(*e*) Proportion.
(*f*) Interest, discount, Savings' Banks and Consols.
(*g*) Elementary mensuration.

Grammar, Recitation, and English Literature.
To discuss in the class a subject introduced by the examiner.
Declamation of a speech.
Historical grammar.

Geography.
Position of the earth and moon in the Solar System. Eclipses. Latitude and Longitude. Figure of the earth. Tides; Trade-winds; Ocean-currents. Circulation of water on the earth by Evaporation, Dew, Rainfall, Glaciers, Rivers, Seas. Changes of coast-line produced by the action of Water. Hot-springs, Earthquakes and Volcanos.

Explanation of terms necessarily occurring in connection with the above subjects.

English History.
The growth of the Colonial power of the British Empire, and the loss of the American Colonies.

General Remarks explanatory of suggested Scheme of Instruction in Science.

The obstacles in the way of teaching the Elements of Science in Elementary Schools do not arise from any inherent difficulty in the subject, so much as from its mere want of familiarity. Until the object to which a scientific statement relates is sufficiently well known for the terms used in referring to it to call up a clear conception in the learner's mind, it is impossible for the statement itself to be understood and firmly grasped. If remembered at all, it is remembered simply as a phrase to which no definite meaning is attached. This is the chief reason why what ought to be pre-eminently a knowledge of things, is often much more truly a mere knowledge of words about things than knowledge which a child gets from any other part of its school training.

As the most effectual way of securing results of real value from the time and labour bestowed upon the teaching of Science in Elementary Schools, it is suggested that in Infant Schools and in the Standards I., II. and III., systematic Object Lessons should be given, which should lead up to more specific scientific instruction to be given in the higher Standards. In these Lessons the aim should be to widen the children's physical experience, and to accustom them to understand and use the terms by which the results of that experience can be accurately expressed. The objects and phenomena forming the starting-point of the scientific instruction to be given in the higher Standards would thus be familiar to the children, and the language in which this instruction was conveyed would be intelligible to them.

For the purposes in view it is considered essential that the Object Lessons here suggested should have reference to three main divisions of knowledge, which may be thus stated:

 A. *Shape and Size*, and properties of bodies depending on them; leading on, in the higher Standards, to Descriptive and Practical Geometry and Mensuration.

 B. *Properties of Matter*, including a knowledge of the more obvious qualities of the materials and implements used in domestic life and in common trades; leading on, in the higher Standards, to the fundamental principles of Mechanics and the rudiments of Physics and Chemistry.

 C. *Plants and Animals*, with a knowledge of the practical

purposes which they subserve and the products derived from them for use in domestic life or in common trades; leading on, in the higher Standards, to General Biology and the rudiments of Physiology.

PROPOSED STANDARDS OF EXAMINATION ON APPLIED MATHEMATICS AND SCIENCES.

General Note.—It is to be understood that the object of the instruction here indicated is rather to cultivate in the children geometrical conceptions than to teach them Geometry. They will therefore not be expected to show more than a practical or mechanical acquaintance with the subjects enumerated. Abstract geometrical relations will be introduced only in so far as they may be needful for accuracy of statement.

Second Standard.

Object Lessons. Division A.

Accurate description and discrimination of the square, rectangle, cube. Rectangular prism; circle, cylinder, sphere; semicircle, Hemisphere.

Formation of larger cubes and squares by putting together small cubes and squares.

Formation of *simple* solid or plane figures (i.e. figures without re-entrant angles), by putting together cubes or squares.

Number of small cubes or squares required to make a given simple figure, estimated from the length of edges. Number of cubes required not to exceed 64; number of squares not to exceed 100.

Division B.

Easily observed properties of familiar solid bodies, e.g. weight, hardness, pliability, elasticity, tenacity. Common processes in which these properties are exhibited.

The children should be able to give examples of the selection of materials for familiar uses, because of the great or small degree in which they possess such properties.

Division C.

Children to enumerate animals known to them, and give reasons why they class them together. The same with plants. The same with mineral bodies.

Common materials used in domestic life or in well-known trades to be referred to their origin from animals, plants or minerals.

Third Standard.

Object Lessons. Division A.

Simple cases of the generation of plane figures by sections of solids; as the square, rectangle, parallelogram, as sections of the square prism; circle and ellipse as sections of cylinder. All plane sections of sphere are circles. A cylinder touches a plane in a line; a sphere touches a plane in a point. Tangent-planes as limiting cases of sectional planes.

Division B.

Distinctive properties of solids, liquids and gases, in relation to shape and bulk.

Further properties of matter: impenetrability. Proofs of impenetrability of air (by diving-bell, &c.).

Degrees of solidity and fluidity: plastic solids, viscid liquids.

Fusibility, solubility, combustibility.

Bending, twisting, stretching, squeezing.

Children to give familiar examples as before.

Division C.

Lessons similar to those of Standard II., going more into detail and including a wider range of objects.

Common materials referred to the particular parts of plants or animals from which they are derived, e.g. tea, coffee, flour, cotton, wool, silk, leather, &c.

Fourth Standard.

Practical Geometry.

Simple cases of the generation of surfaces by the translatory motion of lines; and of solid figures by the translatory motion of surfaces.

Easy cases of the generation of curves other than the circle by simple mechanical means, e.g. ellipse, cycloid.

Mechanics, with Rudiments of Physics and Chemistry.

Weight in connection with bulk: specific gravity, or heaviness. Simple methods of finding the bulk of irregular solids (e.g. immersion in water contained in a glass vessel, and noting how much the surface of the water is raised).

Subjects of Standards II. and III. continued.

General Biology and Physiology.

General characteristics of animals and plants continued.

Habits of less common animals or plants.

Common processes of manufacture applied to products obtained from plants or animals.

[Advantage should here be taken of any local trade with which the majority of the children may be supposed to be more or less familiar.]

Fifth Standard.

Practical Geometry.

Simple cases of the generation of surfaces of revolution.

Solids of revolution generated by revolution of rectangle, circle, or other simple closed plane figures about an axis in their own plane. Cylinder and cone generated by motion of a straight line.

Areas of rectangles, parallelograms and triangles to be estimated from measurements of bases and altitudes, results to be verified by folding or cutting figures drawn on paper.

Mechanics, with Rudiments of Physics and Chemistry.

Matter of all kinds resists change of motion.

Resistance to change of motion, considered as a property of which bodies may have more or less, is *inertia*. Whatever can overcome inertia, and so change motion, is *force*. Weight considered as a force.

Rate of motion : *velocity*.

Quantity of motion : *momentum*.

Work done in raising heavy bodies. Working power of falling water, &c.

Equality of work of power and weight in "Simple Machines" in equilibrium and without friction.

Reference to familiar examples whenever possible.

General Biology and Physiology.

Broad outlines of the life-history of a flowering plant. Structure and functions of its principal parts, as root, stem, leaves, flower, &c. Comparative examination of a few common, well-marked species.

Broad outlines of the structure and functions of a vertebrated animal, with special reference to man : food, breathing, digestion, circulation, removal and replacement of waste material.

Sixth Standard.

Practical Geometry.

Simple construction with straight-edge and set-square.

Method of assigning points by reference to two fixed axes at right angles. Children to lay down points thus on squared paper (architects' "section paper," or a "cross-ruled" exercise-book). The straight line as *locus* of points fulfilling the common condition $y = a + bx$.

Volume of rectangular solids from linear dimensions.

Mechanics, with Rudiments of Physics and Chemistry.

Subjects of Standard V. continued.

Very simple numerical examples on motion with uniform and uniformly *accelerated* velocity.

Rectilinear motion of bodies under influence of gravity.

Pressure in liquids and gases.

Distinctive properties of solids, liquids and gases, in relation to pressure. Pressure due to weight of liquids and gases.

Floating bodies.

Equilibrium of fluids.

Atmospheric pressure, as illustrated by barometer, pumps, &c.

First notions of Chemistry of Air and Water.

General Biology and Physiology.

Subjects of Standard V. continued and in greater detail: a arger number of species included.

Subjects of Standard V. continued. Animal heat, necessity for clothing; muscular exertion, exhaustion, repose.

Seventh Standard.

Practical Geometry.

Constructions with straight-edge and set-square continued. Curves plotted on squared paper, from equations of first or second degree; also from results of observations accessible to children; e.g. daily or hourly readings of a thermometer hung up in the school-room; or thermometric or barometric readings given in the daily paper; or of the height of the end-points of minute and hour hands of school clock above lowest point of clock face, from measurements taken every five minutes.

Easy calculations of areas and volumes involving knowledge of area of circle in terms of radius.

Mechanics, with Rudiments of Physics and Chemistry.

Force estimated numerically by the rate at which it can generate momentum.

Numerical measure of force due to weight of a pound or other known mass.

Energy. Work in wider sense. Loss of mechanical energy by friction, &c. Mechanical equivalent of heat.

Temperature: thermometer. Measurement of heat. Expansion, fusion, evaporation.

Chemistry of Air and Water more fully.

Combustion of ordinary fuel, oxidation of common metals.

Alkalis and commonest acids and salts.

General Biology and Physiology.

Subjects of Standard V. continued and in greater detail: a larger number of species included.

Subjects of Standards V. and VI. continued.

Nervous system.

Sensory and motor nerves.

Glance at animal kingdom in general.

Fourth Schedule.

Geometry. *First Stage.*

Properties of angles between two straight lines: properties of triangles as far as they can be demonstrated without the introduction of parallels.

Algebra.

The sole axiom in Arithmetic and Algebra, that the value of a number is independent of the order in which the units are counted.

Addition. Proof of $a + b = b + a$.
$$a + (b + c) = (a + b) + c$$
$$= a + b + c.$$

Subtraction. Proof of $a - (b + c) = a - b - c$.
$$a - (b - c) = a - b + c.$$
Exercises in the above.

Multiplication. Proof of $ab = ba$.
$$a(bc) = (ab)c = abc.$$
$$a(b + c) = ab + ac.$$
$$a(b - c) = ab - ac.$$
Exercises in the above.

Geometry. *Second Stage.*

Theory of parallels: parallelograms: areas of triangles and parallelograms: transformation to equivalent areas: squares on sides of a right-angled triangle.

Algebra.

Introduction of negative quantities. Generalizations of the notions involved in the symbols $+$, $-$, and $=$. Addition, Subtraction and Multiplication of negative quantities.

Division as inverse of Multiplication.

Quotients as Fractions.

Proof of $\dfrac{a}{b} \times c = \dfrac{ac}{b}$ $\qquad \dfrac{a}{b} \div c = \dfrac{a}{bc}$

$\qquad \dfrac{a}{b} = \dfrac{am}{bm}$ $\qquad \dfrac{a}{b} \times \dfrac{c}{d} = \dfrac{ac}{bd}$

$\qquad \dfrac{a}{b} \div \dfrac{c}{d} = \dfrac{ad}{bc}$ $\qquad \dfrac{a}{b} \pm \dfrac{c}{d} = \dfrac{ad \pm bc}{bd}$

Exercises in the above.

Simple Equations of one unknown quantity and problems producing them.

Third Stage.

The circle: the straight line in connection with the circle: angles in a circle.

Note.—These subjects should be taught by oral lessons only. Geometry should be commenced a year earlier than Algebra.

Memorandum.—Latin, French and German have not been dealt with by the Memorialists, for want of time.

www.ingramcontent.com/pod-product-compliance
Lightning Source LLC
Chambersburg PA
CBHW030259170426
43202CB00009B/802